Jim Burson
9-24-14

THE GOLDEN
WHISTLE

D1473716

Praise for *The Golden Whistle*

"*The Golden Whistle* is the best blueprint for success that a young coach could ever have, and the best I have seen in 35 years of searching for one. But really, it is much more than that. It gave this veteran coach reminders of what is important for building and maintaining a program focused on success on and off the court. In addition, I have taken new ideas from *The Golden Whistle* that I can use immediately to improve the educational process for my guys.

Dr Jim Burson has taken the knowledge and experience of a 45-season Hall of Fame coaching career, combined it with the expertise of the classroom professor that he is, and written a masterpiece for educators focused on growing young minds. It is applicable to any sport, or for any educator.

Yellow highlighters were invented for books like *The Golden Whistle*. It has me soul-searching and having thoughts toward self-improvement, not only as I strive to earn my own "Golden Whistle," but more importantly, as I assist the youngsters I coach in earning theirs."

—**Page Moir,** President,
National Association of Basketball Coaches (NABC);
Head Coach, Roanoke College Men's Basketball

"For all coaches out there, this book is a must-read."

—**John Calipari**, Head Coach,
University of Kentucky Men's Basketball

"Your book is terrific, which I knew it would be. Your great love and knowledge of the game come together and provide the secrets to achieving success in coaching and in life. You've done a masterful job of coaching all of us. Well done!"

—**Mike Krzyzewski**, Head Coach,
Duke University Men's Basketball

"Coach Jim Burson has masterfully told a story that illustrates how the game of basketball has evolved and changed through the years, while the values that it teaches remain timeless. The book speaks volumes about the true depth of coaching --- and also the depth of Jim Burson.

The Golden Whistle should be required reading for anyone associated with the profession of coaching regardless of the sport. There is no question that this could double as a textbook for coaches of all ages."

—**Bill Hosket,** Olympic gold medalist, USA Basketball;
former Ohio State University All-American

"This is a unique, well-written story. However, the best of the writing was the invaluable information for all young coaches. A must-read for aspiring young men who think they want to coach."

—**Tates Locke,** collegiate and NBA basketball coach, retired

"What Jim has done with *The Golden Whistle* is to teach us all some very valuable life lessons through the journey of a coach's world. I found it easy to read yet educational at the same time. It's one that I believe many, including me, will re-read. There are that many "golden nuggets" in it!"

—**Kevin Eastman,** Vice President of Basketball Operations,
Los Angeles Clippers

"Your book is making a big difference to me as a parent; thank you for writing it. I'm anxious for other people to have the same experience and for it to change and impact their lives as well."

—**Rebecca Mullen,** basketball mom, Life Coach at http://AltaredSpaces.com

"*The Golden Whistle* is the best manual I have ever read for coaches of any sport. The amazing thing is that the lessons presented are for all coaches regardless of sport, yet they are also for every person. It provides direction for anyone on how to become successful in their area of choice and in life. I wish I had had this book when I first graduated from college, for it would have made me not only a better coach, but a better person. READ IT!"

—**Glenn Wilkes,** National Collegiate Basketball Hall of Fame; Head Coach, Stetson University Men's Basketball (retired)

"Fabulous. Exemplifies what coaching is and why you coach! Coaching U lists this as a MUST-READ for our followers."

—**Brendan Suhr**, Coaching U Live co-founder, NBA (30 years)

THE GOLDEN
WHISTLE

Going Beyond:
The Journey to Coaching Success

JIM BURSON

The Golden Whistle

Copyright © 2014 Exohs LLC

ISBN: 978-0-9960022-0-2

Library of Congress Control Number: 2014936277

Printed in the United States of America

Author photo:
Rod Lang, Muskingum University Public Relations

Cover and Interior Design: Debbie O'Byrne
JETLAUNCH Premium Publishing, www.jetlaunch.net

To the hungry Golden Whistle coaches at all levels who give their time, energy and love to help young people become all they can be. To the great game of basketball that continues to enrich my life every day. The game has blessed me indeed.

CONTENTS

"For the young and dedicated, the ball always bounces up."

—*Author unknown*

FOREWORD

If you are seeking new ways of thinking, teaching and learning the game, I suggest you read *The Golden Whistle*. I believe this book should be essential reading for students and coaches of basketball. This is coaching at its very best.

Jim Burson's path-finding work will greatly influence our understanding of the game and how it can be taught. He showers us with practical insights and common-sense truths that are easy to learn and will produce championship results.

Coach Burson and I have mentored each other for the last thirty-five years. The lessons I've learned from him have positively influenced the way I think, behave and live.

George Raveling

Director of International Basketball, Nike

John W. Bunn Lifetime Achievement Award
Naismith Basketball Hall of Fame

National Collegiate Basketball Hall of Fame

http://www.CoachGeorgeRaveling.com

CHAPTER 1
THE DECISION

Monday Morning

*M*y, *how things have changed over the past forty years,* Coach Faylor thought as he walked out of the shower and stopped long enough to look at his aging face. The hair that he saw in the mirror was completely white and wrinkles creased his face. *Too many bad calls,* he thought to himself, and grinned.

He was amazed at how well his body had held up and thankful for his many years of working out almost every day and watching what he ate. Fortunately, he realized at an early age that these good habits, along with no drinking and no smoking, went a long way toward maintaining good health. However, he was all too aware of his one major health problem—a bad heart with a pacemaker and seven stents. The weak ticker wasn't apparent as he looked in the mirror, but his body still knew it was about time to get off the stress-mobile!

A product of heredity. At least, that's what the doctors said. He remembered the old smoke-filled house with mom and dad both smoking, and seven children around a potbellied coal stove. It may not have been a healthy environment, but it was always full of love.

Faylor smiled as he looked around the coaches' lounge area and reflected back to that old high school office and shower area where he began. The smell of old socks and practice gear permeated everything. One small desk and a straight-back wooden chair faced one wall. A single shower adjoined the office, and water streamed under the door into the office with each use. An overhead lightbulb turned on and off by pulling on a dangling string. Its dingy light merely highlighted the old paint on the walls and worn floorboards. But it was his first office, and he had been so proud.

It almost seemed like a dream.

After Faylor finished dressing, he walked through the door to the players' lounge area and, as always, was struck by the luxury: multiple TVs, beautiful leather lounge chairs, a game area, individualized lockers with pictures and nameplates adorning the fronts. The lockers even had individual air conditioning. An adjoining video area had large screen TVs and soft-armed viewing chairs with the seniors' seats in the front. Everything was so neat and in its place: Nike shoes rested on each stool and practice uniforms all hung in perfect order inside the lockers. He remembered the days of the old Chuck Taylor Converse shoes: black or white; high or low were the only choices.

The video equipment made him think of his playing days when only 8mm and 16mm film existed. It seemed just like yesterday when one mailed out the film and it wouldn't be back for a couple of days. He recalled the black and white short shorts that players wore in his day and how he and his teammates thought they were really big time. The two hand set shot and the underhand foul shots were being taught, but somebody by the name of Kenny Sailors had started shooting a jump shot.

As Faylor walked through the lounge and reflected, he fingered the gold coach's whistle that always hung around his neck. Everyone who knew him knew the whistle, with its unusual color; it had been the subject of innumerable conversations, speculations and press articles throughout his career.

Faylor was jolted back to reality as he walked down the tunnel and into the mammoth 23,500-seat arena and on to the court bearing his name. *Did all of this really happen?* he thought to himself, not for the first time. *It's gone so fast and it seems just a moment ago when I was hired and walked into the old memorial building and thought, 'It just can't get any better than this' and every day it did.* He snapped his fingers and smiled.

Two campus policemen waved at him and asked if they could help him with anything. He was amazed to think that someone was on duty twenty-four hours a day just for building security. The equipment manager (who seemed to have been born here, although actually he had been here 'only' fifty-one years) waved and said that everything was ready for practice. 'Ribs' was a legend on campus and recently inducted into the university's hall of fame. There was no more loyal fan than Ribs. *Will I miss the games and practices?* thought Faylor. *Yes, but it will be the great people, like Ribs, who I will miss the most.*

"Morning, Coach." The words carried distinctly across the cavernous arena. Faylor looked toward the opposite end of the arena and saw Kobert, his long-time associate head coach whom Faylor affectionately called Big K. Kobert waved and smiled as they walked toward each other and met near center court. "Why did you want to meet me here? What's happening?"

Faylor's eyes traveled over the familiar figure as they drew near each other. Kobert was still a huge man. When he played basketball in the '50s, he was a six foot five inch giant who loved to play the game. He was also a great golfer, but his high school didn't have a golf team, for which Faylor was eternally grateful, because Kobert probably would have gone into golf instead of basketball. Kobert and Faylor were teammates throughout their junior high, high school and college careers. Kobert married his high school sweetheart right after high school. They were in an automobile accident on their honeymoon, and she was killed. Kobert never remarried and the pain and loss never left him. But he had been the best friend and assistant coach that anyone could ever have. Faylor called him the real head coach and felt blessed to have had him by his side throughout their careers.

Faylor picked up a ball off the rack and tossed it toward Kobert who caught it, faked a shot and took a quick dribble. "I still have it, Coach," exclaimed Kobert, and then winced as he felt a sharp arthritic pain in his shoulder. "What's on tap for the day? I may be getting up in years but I'm still excited about working on the game today."

"How many years have we shared together?" Faylor asked.

"Well," said Kobert, "counting the fact we played together in high school and college and coaching, about forty-five years. We've lost a little quickness but not our enthusiasm for the game."

"How many championships, how many games have we won together?" continued Faylor. "That's a great question," Kobert responded. "Almost 800 games here alone and if you add high school maybe more than that. We have lots of trophies and we had lots of great times. Why so many questions?"

"We've had a great run together and you've been loyal beyond my wildest expectations. I've received a lot of awards and recognition but you have been the real air in the ball. I want to be sure I tell you exactly how much you have meant to me," said Faylor.

"Wait a minute," Kobert interrupted. "What are you trying to tell me?"

"I think it's time," said Faylor quietly.

"Time for what?"

"Time to find a replacement."

"Why would you do that? Is your heart acting up again?"

"No, but people say you just know and I know it's time."

Kobert pushed the point. "We had a great year last year—thirty plus wins and a Final Four appearance. Our top players are returning this year and we have a great recruiting class. We could win it all one more time."

"Believe me, Big K, I realize that, but it's time. I have spoken to you on many, many occasions about becoming the head coach and now I'm asking you one more time: the job is yours if you want it, along with the ten Golden Nuggets that go with the position."

Kobert was silent for a long moment. He took a deep breath and in a steady voice replied, "No, I haven't changed my mind. I will retire when you go. I guess I'm just a little shocked and disappointed by the timing of your decision." He took a couple of steps toward the ball rack, scooped up the ball Faylor had thrown at him, and replaced it on the rack.

Faylor reached out and gently grasped Kobert by the arm. "Big K, you have been the best friend and colleague I could have ever had. I had a feeling that this would be your answer and I took the liberty of preparing a few surprises for you. I know that your retirement account is healthy and that you are a multi-millionaire from your TIAA-CREF retirement holdings. It makes me smile to say that."

"I never did quite understand your passion for golf," Faylor continued, "but it pleases me a great deal that it brings you such joy. The boosters have paid off your condo in Sarasota and purchased you a lifelong membership at the Stoneybrook golf club there. You'll also maintain your membership at our local course, Eaglesticks, so that you can play wherever you are."

The long-time friends looked at each other and smiled.

They knew each other so well that there was no need for further discussion.

"Who are you thinking of as a replacement?" asked Kobert as Faylor said, "Then let's talk about my replacement." They laughed. Not for the first time, their minds had moved on at the same moment and in the same direction. "You go first," said Kobert.

"This won't come as a total surprise to you," said Faylor, "because we've talked about this many times. Big K, is Little K ready for the big time?"

"He's certainly worked hard as our top assistant over the past five years," replied Kobert, "and before that, when he was a student assistant, we agreed that he was the best ever. Of course, he has just the two years of head coaching and that was at the high school level, which didn't end with a very good record. But as you know, Kichael is tremendously gifted in handling players, relating well to people, and communicating with young people. After all these years, he knows our program inside and out. He's our top recruiter, which is hugely important. Then there were Jackson and Reilly who went on to the first round NBA draft. And our graduation rates are higher than ever."

Kobert scratched the side of his nose, the habit that indicated he was in deep thought. "Yes, Coach, he's ready."

"All right, then, that's settled. I'll talk to the athletic director this afternoon," said Faylor. He continued, "Big K, do you remember that over forty years ago I asked you the same question: was I ready for the big time? You told me I was ready because I was more concerned with learning, with teaching, with making the players better than I was about winning."

As they talked, they walked slowly toward the south end of the arena toward the exit. Faylor continued, "I remember telling you that we needed to treat everyone with kindness, even the officials, the angry fans, and the overzealous alumni magnate—and you agreed with me. I believe that this is one of the reasons that our partnership has been so successful all these years; we share the same human values.

"Well, I must admit that often I was able to do this only because you had my back—you have been my counsel and my rock. And I know I slipped once in a while—remember the chair incident? But the technicals became fewer and fewer over the years.

"Do you remember the mother who was angry with me because her son had not started and how she told me off after the game? I smiled and startled her by kissing her on the cheek and saying, 'I love your son.'"

"Yes," said Kobert, "And she became an executive of our booster club."

"How about the ten years that I wore a brown suit to every single game? There you were in your Armani suits and you still put up with me and supported my idiosyncrasy."

Kobert interrupted and said, "I still don't understand how in the heat of late games that you could maintain your calm demeanor, especially when you got on the players so hard during practice. It was a marvel to observe. I suppose that hanging onto your rolled up program the way you did helped defuse some of the stress."

Kobert continued, "I have to tell you that I thought you'd really lost it when you wrote the series of books about a young player. How on earth would you have the time to write books? But I have to hand it to you —they were great."

Kobert's words tumbled out as memories came flooding back. "Remember, Coach, you were the first to change a game time for ESPN and you were also the first coach willing to be interviewed at half-time. Plus, you're the last of the Division I coaches to teach as well as coach. As I understand it from our student assistants, your 'Principles' class is still legendary among first-year students. I doubt that many university professors before or since use a simple child's song to help students really understand the concept of self-motivation. In fact, just last year the players started singing 'Row, Row, Row Your Boat' on one of the game trips! You always had a traditional, disciplined approach to the classroom and yet have always had the ability to accept and embrace change. I think the students understand that and respect you for it."

"Thanks, Big K. I've tried hard to follow the basic principles that I feel, if studied and learned, can make anyone a great coach." With his typical discomfort in dwelling on his accomplishments, Faylor changed the subject. "So you really think that Little K has done his homework and is ready?"

They opened the arena door and stepped out into a beautiful sunny day. "Yes, Coach, I believe no one is more prepared than he is."

"Big K, your friendship is one of my greatest assets. That's why I wanted to meet with you today. I trust no one's judgment like I trust yours. How should we proceed once I've spoken to the AD? Will you help me prepare to make the announcement? What are the proper steps to take? Time is a precious commodity and my time in coaching is running out, as is yours—but Little K's hourglass is just starting to be filled."

Kobert turned his head to hide sudden tears. He and Coach Faylor were not accustomed to demonstrating emotion with each other. In an unsteady voice he replied, "Thank you for giving me the opportunity to coach with you. It has been a pleasure and a joy to stand beside the greatest coach in the world."

Faylor nodded his head and patted his friend's elbow, unwilling to risk his own voice to reply in words. Then in characteristic 'get it done' fashion, he said, "Let's go find Little K and see what he thinks. He should be ready and I doubt that he will be surprised."

Coach Faylor snapped his fingers and the two men headed toward the administration wing.

CHAPTER 2
THE ANNOUNCEMENT

Tuesday Morning

How quickly the news travels these days, thought Faylor. *The sports channel here on campus had rumors last night that I might retire and ESPN already started talking about it this morning. I've already had an amazing number of e-mails wanting to know more about the position and it hasn't even been announced.*

He smiled to himself, as memories of past games and former players ran through his mind, triggered by the phone calls he had received from astonished former players wanting to know if the rumor was true—all asking, "Are you really hanging it up, Coach?" Several asked whether the next coach would automatically get Faylor's golden whistle. Of course, they laughed about the legend of the golden whistle.

Kobert had left him a message confirming that the official announcement would be made this afternoon at two o'clock and that proper protocol had already begun.

Faylor sighed. He knew all too well what that meant. It was important, but tedious: fair labor laws, a national job search and carefully-worded formal announcements. This would take time but the search would start immediately, and it would be done the right way. But Faylor was pulling for Little K in a big way. It was done—indeed! And his own coaching days were over.

As Faylor entered the arena to meet with Kobert, he felt a twinge of sadness at the thought of never coaching again. Last year at this time he was excited about preparing for the off-season and today he was preparing for a new life.

In response to Faylor's questioning look, Kobert said, "The ball is in the air. The news will hit all the major outlets today. Candidates are already throwing their hats into the hoop. Of course, a three million dollar-plus salary would be attractive to a lot of people," he smiled.

The two walked past the drinking fountain and looked up at the life-sized picture of Faylor. "It always embarrasses me a little to see that picture," explained Faylor, "not so much because it's me, but because there's not a picture of you there with me. Yes, I need to look into that."

"Don't be ridiculous, Coach. All I did was ride on the coat-tails of one of the great minds in the history of the game. I don't need a picture, I know I'm there. Thank you again for the great trip!"

Faylor let it go for the moment. "Come with me into my office. I want to show you something," he said, and the two old friends climbed the steps that led to the corridor where his corner office was located. The office itself looked like something from a movie—brass-trimmed leather furniture, polished mahogany desk and tables—everything carefully selected and designed to impress the greatest of recruits. Kobert had never gotten used to the grandeur of his friend's office. *No one has better facilities*, he thought. *I was stunned the first time I walked into this room. I was humbled and proud,*

*excited and perplexed. Never in my wildest dreams could I have
imagined an office like this.*

Faylor's voice interrupted Kobert's reverie. "Big K, you
were present when I received my golden whistle so many years
ago. Like many people, you know there are coaching secrets
associated with that whistle. Now the time has come for me
to tell you the whole story.

"When the great Coach Aupp gave me the whistle, he
also entrusted me with a set of handwritten notebooks con-
taining the golden nuggets of basketball coaching that he had
gathered over the years. He told me how these secret notebooks came to be. It's an amazing story, and I need to go back
to Aupp's youth to tell it.

"Coach Aupp always said that he was lucky to have
coached in the twenties, during the early stages of the development of the game. He told me that he fell in love with basketball at age six, when his mom stuffed rags into a gunny sack
and sewed it up into a ball. She then helped him make a hoop
out of a clothes hanger with pieces of rag tied onto the make-
shift rim. He even made balls out of pieces of paper taped
together with masking tape." The two men shook their heads
at the thought of the motivation and ingenuity involved.

"He also told me that he spent a lot of time thinking
about the game even as a kid and asked questions of anyone
he could, which wasn't received very well on his family farm.
However, his dad once took him to see the Hilliard Compa-
ny's AAU team play. Even then, forty years later, I believed
him when he said that was one of the best days of his life. I
could see his eyes shine at the memories.

"Aupp played in high school and then was fortunate to
play at the University of Kansas for Dr. Forest 'Phog' Allen,
who we now know as the father of basketball coaching. He
made it a point to meet and get to know Dr. James Naismith,
creator of basketball, who had founded the Kansas program
and was then the athletic director for the Jayhawks. He told

me that Naismith loved answering his questions about the brief history and development of the game and what Naismith envisioned for the future."

Coach Faylor continued, "Coach Aupp was the first to admit that he was never a great player, but he was a devoted student of the game and became a great coach, helping Naismith and Allen. He told me that at that time, a lot of other coaches would visit Kansas to talk basketball and learn from the great Phog Allen, and Aupp did his best to sit in on these conversations as much as possible."

"Boy, would I like to have been a little mouse in the corner and listen to those conversations," exclaimed Big K. Coach Faylor looked at him and saw that twinkle of excitement in his eye. He then reached back to the shelf behind him, picked up an old ball, and tossed it at Big K, who caught it with the laces up. They both smiled as they thought about the fact that the ball actually had laces!

Coach Faylor grinned at his friend and then returned to his story. "Many of these visitors were an amazing 'who's who' of coaching for the next generation. John Bunn, assistant to Coach Allen and later the coach at Stanford, was a leader in the scientific aspects of coaching. Doc Carlson, who coached at the University of Pittsburgh for thirty-one years, amazed everyone by showing the 'figure 8' offense that he had invented. Everett Dean visited; he coached at Indiana and Stanford. He was one of the great gentlemen of the game, won the national title in 1942 and talked about the philosophy of what it takes to be a coach. Bruce Drake, who was coaching at Oklahoma at the time, created 'the Drake Shuffle,' a magnificent continuity offense that was way ahead of the game at that time."

"Is that like the shuffle we ran in high school?" interjected Big K? "It sure is," replied Faylor.

Faylor continued. "Coach Aupp told me that one day Dr. Allen came to him and said, 'Hey, can you help me out with something on the QT?

'Sure!' Aupp responded.

"Allen continued, 'You know that Coach Naismith doesn't believe that basketball should be coached, but I can tell that good coaching is going to be the key to the success of this new sport. So I've been collecting lots of great nuggets of information on coaching. They need to be put together, edited and sequenced and placed in chapters so they can be taught more efficiently. I know that you're really good at this kind of thing. Will you help me create some notebooks on coaching basketball? But remember, we can't tell Naismith about this. He'd have a fit.

"Allen went on. 'I have a young student assistant by the name of John McLendon, who loves basketball and who I think will someday be a great coach. He said he'd be glad to help you with this project.'"

Big K inquired, "Is that the same John McLendon who came to our first practice for years with his beautiful wife Joanna?" Faylor nodded. Big K said, "We always went to Adornetto's for pizza and played the Love Machine. His wife laughed out loud when John hit the button that said, "Poor fishy. Try again." after she had hit the top button that said, "Unbelievable lover."

Faylor replied, "Yes, Coach Aupp introduced me to John when I was a young coach and for some reason Coach McLendon took me under his wing and always kept up with my career. He and I remained friends until his death. It all started with the coaching notebook project that those two worked on for 'Phog' Allen.

"McLendon helped out for the first year, but after that," continued Faylor, "compiling these notebooks became Coach Aupp's life's work along with his coaching career. He started gathering information and followed a simple process of reading, writing and filing all the information he could get. This developed into a set of ten notebooks that he called the 'Ten Golden Nuggets,' which were his solutions to make this great game even better. He developed a process that taught him the habit of constant learning.

"When Coach entrusted me with the notebooks and the golden whistle, he also said, 'As with every important privilege, there are responsibilities. In addition to maintaining the integrity of the nuggets, keeping their legacy alive and adding your own insights along the way as the game evolves, you must mentor and groom other coaches throughout your career, watching for the one with the right qualities to be your successor, someone who would truly make the most of the nuggets and earn his own golden whistle.'" Faylor's voice trailed off as he was once again reminded of just how much his life had changed since he first received the golden whistle and the nuggets. He shook his head, straightened his shoulders, took a breath and continued.

"I've added my insights to the nuggets over the years in sections called 'From the Office.' How long do you think it took to type them out for the computer? I did this in order to protect the original handwritten notebooks, which had become worn with study, handling and age.

"Over the past several weeks I've had a wonderful time reviewing the original notebooks from start to finish, re-reading my favorite parts and making final changes to my own additions. Just this morning my secretary finished the updates and placed all the files on this flash drive."

He waved the small electronic device in the air. "Look at this. Can you believe it? I hold all the secrets of coaching on this little piece of metal. It boggles my mind how far we have come in the past fifty years. Remember the old mimeograph machines that got that awful purple stuff on your hands? What will the future bring?" The two men laughed ruefully, as they had shared many struggles in mastering even the basics of ever-changing technology in recent years. It all came so easily to the younger coaches and student assistants, who knew that tech support for the two senior coaches was part of their job descriptions.

"Are you curious to see the nuggets, Big K? You know most of the information even better than I do. You have become a golden whistle coach."

Big K was enthralled and impatient to learn even more. "What a question! All I wanted to do was help you and the team. Keep talking, my friend."

Faylor nodded. "It's true there has been much guessing about what allowed us to win so many games and much speculation about the secret that I possessed. I hate to burst everyone's bubble, but the secret is that there really is not just one secret. Study the game, take time to engage and learn the nuggets and make those nuggets your own. Anyone willing to put in the time and effort can master the principles that are on this flash drive. These are the secrets. Oh yes, there's one more secret," he said in a secretive voice. "**It helps to have good players!**" They both chuckled.

"These nuggets are the core principles of my own philosophy of the game. As I learned them and made them my own, I called my philosophy Solution-Based Basketball. As you know, this is the name of our award-winning coaching development program. Do you remember how elated I was when I learned that we had been awarded trademark protection for the term Solution-Based Basketball? That's because the term is deeply personal to me. I help coaches find and create their own solutions."

"You have always been so willing to share your knowledge with anyone who would ask," said Kobert. "You must have been tempted to give out the notebooks at times."

"Yes, occasionally," replied Faylor. "But I really had no choice. When I accepted the notebooks with the golden nuggets, I also agreed to honor the promise I made Coach Aupp to only give them to the right person.

"Coach Aupp knew even before I did that I would apply all the nuggets and become the best I could become. He knew that I would accept the challenge, that I would read and deeply study each nugget. He knew that I would apply each principle from the nuggets over time so that each one would become part of my inner being. I guess if you win nearly 800 games you always think you've done a great job, but I could have been better.

"Coach Aupp told me that a lot of young coaches learn bits and pieces of nuggets as they progress through their career—some even figure out all the nuggets on their own; but very few spend the time or energy to earn the golden whistle and make the nuggets their own. And he was right. I'm not the only coach with this knowledge. I've known junior high coaches who have vicariously earned golden whistles just by giving their heart to the game. They didn't win 800 games, but they helped make their players better in all ways.

"A coach may not win an NCAA title or 800 games or be named national coach of the year or be selected to the Naismith Hall of Fame. But you can make a difference every day and touch the lives of all the players you coach and students you teach. These golden moments turn your whistle to gold. Thank you again for helping me develop Solution-Based Basketball, Kobert."

Kobert reached out and grasped his friend's arm. He knew that Faylor addressed him with his given name only on the most momentous occasions, and he was deeply moved emotionally. He wanted to say 'thank you,' but his voice cracked and he felt a tear roll off his cheek.

Faylor felt the moment, then continued. "Coach Aupp told me that one day someone would show himself to me and that I would recognize that this person would be my golden whistle successor. You know I would have loved to have you be that coach, but you have always wanted to remain with me as my assistant coach. And you have been the best. You've earned the assistant coach golden whistle through your love, your loyalty and your own gifts. And I also understand why you will retire with me. Kobert, you have blessed me indeed.

"So I have waited patiently and I think Little K is the answer. He has shown by his love of his players and his commitment to the truth that he possesses the characteristics to become a great coach. I think he is ready. Five years ago, when he joined our staff after his trial by fire as a high school coach, I entrusted the golden nuggets to him. All this time he has studied the nuggets, the game and the Solution-Based Basketball process and is making them his own. I think he is ready for his golden whistle. He was by far the best student assistant we've ever had. He got baptized by fire in his two years as a high school coach. He has studied the nuggets and shows maturity beyond his years. I hope; no, I think; no, I **know** he's ready.

"Coach Aupp said that it would be my choice to whom and how I wanted to pass on the nuggets. I thought about it for a long time before deciding to put the nuggets on this flash drive. This was a big decision, because it would open the secrets to everyone. The game of basketball has changed so much—long pants, fancy dunks, overplay defense, millionaire players. Technology has expanded access to everyone's coaching information. Our world is so complex, and the information the nuggets contain is so important that I want them to reach many more people.

"Today, anyone who wants to be a coach can find just about anything on the internet. But how does he or she know which information is accurate, helpful or most effective? The nuggets have been curated and developed over time by experienced professionals in the game; they are reliable and trustworthy and will lead coaches who want to learn along a productive coaching path. With these notebooks, a smart learner-coach can cut through the chaos of internet information and find the true nuggets that will help. I know that Little K will be a principled guardian of the nuggets and understand how to wisely use the wonders of digital communication to share the wisdom of the nuggets.

"But just because the information is available doesn't mean that many coaches will earn a golden whistle. Very few will dig long enough or deep enough to mine enough nuggets to become a great coach. A lot will know the X's and O's, but very few will study the inner game of basketball—the Invisible Vision.

"Little K has shown great insight and maturity. He is bright and he has great relationship skills. It won't be easy for him, but he has the right stuff.

"To become a great coach is never easy. It carries a price in time and effort, both mentally and physically. It must be developed daily with self-discipline, self-awareness, hard work and patience. Like knowledge, it has to be sought out, developed and constantly improved upon. If you want your players tough, the coach must be tough and see things others just don't see.

"But anyone who aspires to greatness will have a chance. It is never easy to become the best. A lot of people want instant success and will take shortcuts to get there, but you and I know you can't build a career on shortcuts.

"So, my friend, there is no genius standing here beside you. Only a coach who has dedicated his life to being the best coach he can possibly become. The many times you wondered why we did certain things, the times you even questioned my sanity, were not the results of a stress-filled coach but the result of the application of the golden nuggets that I followed every day. I was developing my own solution-based basketball process by reading and studying the nuggets and applying them to my own style of coaching.

"The style of play, the seven different offenses, the variation of defenses, sometimes possession by possession, which about drove you nuts, were really guided by the principles. It was not so much what we did but how we did it that made us successful and each decision was not through my wisdom but through the application of the ten nuggets."

"But there really is a secret!" interrupted Kobert. "It lies in each coach's application of the ten nuggets. You must not only read and study the ten nuggets, but you must engage them daily, develop your own philosophy of the game and never quit learning—that is Solution-Based Basketball and that is what you've taught all these years."

Faylor nodded in agreement and replied, "Yes. It's all in the nuggets. You must study each nugget and practice the secret of each one. The first nugget explains the Big Word Offense. You must master and engage your words before going on to the next.

"I remember using the book *Word Power Made Easy* to improve the players' vocabulary. Some really got it; some thought it a waste of time. Little K was unbelievable with the book. He learned every word from cover to cover, even adding some of his own words, comments and insights. He would then come to my office to challenge me. He even tried to trick me by asking me a word that wasn't in the book. It didn't work. He showed great leadership for the members of the team and they were also amazed.

"The way Little K engaged and absorbed that book was my first hint that he might be a worthy successor for the nuggets. Anyone who engages, internalizes and personalizes these principles has the power to accumulate all the wins he desires. Ironically, because of his acquired understanding, he will no longer desire wins. Instead, he will only want to become the best he can be. Others may anoint him with a golden whistle long before he really deserves one, because he happened to win.

"That might be the truth we all seek–to become the best you can become is more important than the number of wins. The real aim of coaching is to help players help themselves to become great.

"The nuggets must be read and engaged in the proper sequence. Each one is numbered. Part of the discipline that you acquire by following this process will help you become a great coach. It has been said that things that are invisible are the most powerful. So it will be as you develop your own Invisible Vision: powerful invisible traits of discipline, fortitude, courage and toughness. These words are part of the Big Word Offense that we taught every day and which is also the first nugget.

"This is a task that anyone can master but very few will. The great challenge is in mental toughness and the habits you acquire while mining the nuggets. There are no shortcuts. There must be a price in time and concentration until each nugget becomes a part of your personality, until each nugget becomes a habit of living.

"Countless coaches have approached players as though they had a beating stick in their hand. They used that 'stick' when players made mistakes, then watched as the team died from trying to be perfect. Never punish a player who wants to get better. I **love** Solution-Based Basketball."

"It all makes sense now," Kobert said softly. "I now realize why you guarded the nuggets."

Faylor said, "I have given out portions of the nuggets at clinics, at camps and at seminars. I've never given them all together as I gave them to Little K. I tried to show generosity to all coaches who came to our practices, but I could tell that they came for specific answers to specific topics, and not for the nuggets. I saw a different trait in Little K. He wanted all the knowledge and he seemed to know the nuggets before I had even showed them to him. It almost seemed that he had already read and studied them. I had never seen or felt that trait in anyone else. He really listened and learned during those four years he spent as a manager … oh! I mean as a student assistant. He has earned the right to pursue the golden whistle. Even after he learned the nuggets, he transposed them into his own thoughts and developed his own process based on changing times and circumstances. I love how he added 'From the Locker Room' which follows my own additions, 'From the Office,' and Coach Aupp's section, 'From the Classroom.' I suppose the next additions will be called 'From the Internet.' Can you imagine what the game and the computer will be like by the time Little K retires?"

Kobert gazed in amazement and reached his hand out for Faylor. Again he had to hide the tears. They shook hands. "Thank you again for sharing your coaching with me for the past fifty years—you have blessed me indeed."

They looked at each other and Faylor's mind slipped back seven years to the day that Little K approached him on the quad and the two then talked in his office.

CHAPTER 3
THE CONVERSATION

Seven Years Earlier

Coach Faylor walked across campus and entered the quadrangle with its endless stream of students scurrying to class. "Hi Coach," "Good to see you, Coach," "Hey, Coach, great year," greeted him as he walked toward the arena. He had always loved walking to work. The campus was constantly expanding and the university now had more than 50,000 students; its medical school was the best in the country. Not for the first time Faylor thought, *what a great place to spend my life.*

"Hey, Coach, can I talk to you a moment?" Faylor looked around and saw his star student assistant, George Kichael, whom everyone called Little K. Faylor thought, *he certainly has grown from that scrawny little freshman to a good-looking, very athletic young man.* He remembered Kichael's family life—it was very tough. He lost his mother in the third grade and his dad became surly and abusive, so he lived with his grandparents. His experiences had turned him into a tough-minded yet very kind young man, rare and wonderful qualities to possess.

"Sure, son, how are you doing? You've done a great job as a student assistant the past four years. I'm going to miss that constant smile and unwavering enthusiasm. You've stood out by your effort to help us be the best we could be. What are you going to do with that math and science major?"

"Thanks, Coach," he said as he looked at the ground, a little embarrassed by the compliment. "I want to teach and coach. Coach, you know I want to be a great coach just like you. **I know I can win.** I would like to work for you and stay on your staff, even as a graduate assistant, if this might be possible. **I know I can win.** I want to teach and be a great coach."

"Well, Little K, I don't think we have an opening this year, but I'll look around for you," replied the coach.

"If I can't help you, then I would like to be a head high school coach. I want to show people **I can win.** The players here have been great, but they laugh at me when I tell them I am going to be a great coach someday. I think I'm ready to go earn my golden whistle. **I know I can win.**

"You've been a great teacher, mentor and role model for me. You even gave me my nickname. I want to learn as much as I can and then make it simple to teach and make it my own. I want my own golden whistle and to develop my own solution-based basketball program."

"So you know about the golden whistle?" asked Coach Faylor.

"Yes, sir, everyone talks about it."

Faylor studied Kichael's eager and earnest face and thought, *This just might be the right time and this just may be the person I've been waiting for. There's only one way to find out.*

"Do you have a class this period?"

"No, nothing until eleven."

"Then this is a good time to talk."

He regarded the young man with great seriousness and said, "You talk about wanting to win; however, true winning is of the heart and not in wins and losses, Little K. In order to be a good coach, it's about doing everything you can to become the best you can be and to be able to make the players the best they can be. We've often spoken about Solution-Based Basketball. That's the heart of the concept—finding ways to become the best you can be."

"How can I continue to get better?" exclaimed Little K.

"You've learned this the past four years by sacrificing yourself for the good of the team. You've cleaned the basketballs, washed uniforms, swept and cleaned the floors, helped set up the gym, run the videos, done the stats in practice, all without complaining one time. You have set a great example for all of us to follow and a lot of people have noticed your effort. You may have been 'just' a student assistant, but you have been the best one I've ever had and the best you possibly could be.

"I remember once a player threw up on the floor, and as the trainer was helping the player, you had already gotten extra towels and the bucket and mop and were cleaning it up. After practice I said, 'You might be careful when you do the laundry and keep those towels separate.' You said, 'Thanks, coach; it's already done.' You then told me that the practice tape was all set up for me to watch and asked if you could watch it with me! It was then I first realized that you really wanted to be a basketball coach!

"Now you want more. That's a great thing. The secret of getting more is to be the best you can be where you are today. I will do everything I can to help you achieve your goals but just as you worked hard in the past, you must be prepared to work hard in the future."

"Hi, Coach Faylor. Hey, Little K. How are you doing?" called a cute young coed as she passed by. Coach Faylor looked up and waved at the young woman. Little K seemed embarrassed but he returned her greeting with a rather sheepish smile and then turned back to the older man. "Why is it so hard to coach? It always looked easy for you."

"It was never easy," answered Coach Faylor. "You'll find out quickly how tough it is to be a head coach. When the other teachers are home at night with their families, you will be preparing for the next practice, the next game. You'll be on the road scouting. It's a challenging and lonely path, especially at the beginning. You'll be tempted to give up. This is where you can determine if you really want to earn a golden whistle. It is not about wins, but in learning to do the very best you can, to do things right and to do them with class.

"I know where there is a high school opening. Do you want me to look into this for you?" Little K almost shouted in surprise. "That would be unbelievable." His eyes sparkled with excitement.

"Remember," cautioned Faylor. "If you take this job, you will represent our program, you will represent me, and most important, you will represent yourself. I will be watching. Remember, I expect you to have class.

"Remember this too: There is nothing wrong with trying and failing. Failure comes to everyone who sustains and earns the golden whistle. Obstacles and problems will help you get better—if you accept the challenge. Do you think you can handle this?"

Little K returned Faylor's serious look. "Yes, sir," he replied. "I won't fail. **I know I can win.**"

They had continued walking during the conversation. Faylor looked up and saw the familiar entrance to the athletic facility. "Oh, we've gotten to the arena. Come on up to my office and we'll talk more."

"Do you think I want to win too much?" asked Little K.

"Wins should never be your goal in life. True wealth is of the heart, not in victories." Faylor opened the door to his office, led Kichael in, and motioned him to sit down in the nearby guest chair. "You must strive beyond the winning, beyond the fame. Strive instead for happiness, for satisfaction, to love and be loved, and to acquire peace of mind and serenity."

"Why is wanting to win a bad thing? You can't acquire fame without it," Little K asked in a quiet voice, somewhat intimidated by the surroundings.

Youth never changes, thought Faylor. He shook his head at Kichael and said in mock reproach, "Desire to win for fame and money and not noble ideals have changed this young boy into a mighty man ready to do battle with the best coaches in the world. Good luck with that one." He continued with more patience, "There is much you need to learn about life and about the game and I will help you. But, most importantly, you must help yourself.

"The help I give you will be as a single word in a year of talks compared with the things you must teach yourself. It will not be easy. You must prove yourself. You must find out if you have the fire inside to make yourself a great teacher/coach. This is the basis of coaching and teaching. This is the basis of Solution-Based Basketball: being able to define yourself as a coach. Adding value to the game, to your school, to the players—not winning—is the essence of your golden whistle pursuit.

"I am happy for your ambition, but this is just the beginning. Your words are full of promises, but they must be matched and exceeded by your actions.

"Can you endure the life of a coach? You have a girlfriend. Will she understand? You want to have a family eventually. It will be a great challenge to keep things in perspective."

Little K burst out, "No. I did have a girlfriend but she thought I was crazy to hang around basketball all the time. She broke up with me."

Faylor replied, "Maybe she was not the right one. It takes a special kind of person to be a coach's spouse. My wife has been unbelievable. I am blessed indeed. I find it baffling that she has believed in me and supported me for all these years. She was a piano major with a great music background and her parents taught music, yet she never wavered in her love and support of me as a basketball coach. She seemed content to raise our family and work for the high school as a secretary. Did you know she was inducted into the high school hall of fame? What a great lady. Things have changed, of course, and two-career marriages are the norm. However, no married coach—male or female—can succeed without a supportive spouse." Little K nodded in agreement, although part of him was thinking it might be easier to just remain single his whole life.

Faylor continued his counsel. "The challenge is great and the rewards are tremendous if you are successful. But remember, the rewards are great because so few actually succeed. The obstacles will appear everywhere; there are so many and they are so large that most coaches just give up in despair. You must understand that this is part of coaching. Many see the mermaid's head, but never see the dragon's tail. You can't let yourself be dragged under by the challenges, the criticism and failures you will encounter. You must be able to keep hooked into your goal and stay on your own path.

"Victory that comes easily also goes away easily. The struggle will harden you for the success that will follow. But watch out for fool's gold.

"You see only the mermaid's head and bare bosoms as most people do: all the money, the accolades, the attention, the new home, the possessions, the fans, the cheerleaders." Little K turned red with embarrassment. "These are wonderful, but they cannot interfere with your goal. Coaching can be the loneliest profession in the world. You must find people you can trust, people who share your enthusiasm. Coaching looks good to the average person, but you must understand it is never easy, even when you win. Not in the pros or college or high school or junior high or summer leagues. Not before you win your first game and not after you've won 800 games.

"Your courage and strength of character will be challenged. You will face losses not only of games but also of players, parents, and fans. The ones you trust most will turn on you the quickest. Read the papers and see how quickly it turns. You must be tough. Each disappointment must be overcome. You will want to quit. You will be lonely. You must decide now that you will never give up.

"In your loneliest moments and disappointments you can only survive if you can ask for help. But don't be surprised that in your darkest moments your friends turn away. You must sustain yourself anyway, even in the darkest gyms."

The older coach smiled and said, "You will be filled with doubt. You'll ask yourself why you ever wanted to coach. These moments are the moments of your greatest despair and will prepare you for your greatest victories. Many good coaches have stopped too soon because of feeling lost and lonely or because of anxiety and frustration. You must be able to continue to move in the direction of your goals. Despair is found easily. Dig deep to get beyond it.

"Are you sure you want me to continue, Little K?"

Kichael nodded yes with a shy smile. He knew in his heart that coaching basketball was his destiny. He responded, "I don't know how to explain it, but I have always known that I wanted to coach."

Coach Faylor replied, "The dragon's tail is always there. It might be out of sight just below the surface of the water, but it is always there and you must understand this from the very beginning.

"When you lose, when you win, when you cut players, when you disagree with sports writers, when a parent attacks your character and the fans and newspaper turn on you— then you will know how much you really want to coach. For example, the press can be good, or they can be tough on you. After a close loss last year, I said that I was disappointed in our effort and the players seemed to let down late in the game. The headline read, 'Coach Faylor Gives Up On Team!' The dragon's tail is real and you must learn to handle it.

"You have been a great student of the game. I have watched you take notes and watch videos, but you have just seen the tip of the iceberg. I can see sparks dancing in your eyes. You are glowing with excitement, fired up, full of enthusiasm and purpose, but you have no idea what is about to happen. I am not sure you know what it takes to win. Not now, maybe not ever. You must fill your bags with purposeful preparation."

"I have a friend who is looking for a high school coach who can also teach math. It doesn't pay much and they haven't won many games in the past twenty years. They're still living on the state championship they won nearly forty years ago. The school is in a tiny farm community with people who are not excited about the frivolous nature of basketball. They've gone through eight coaches in the past twenty years. All have been run out of town.

"If you want to be an assistant with me, then you need to go into the world and prove yourself. I will have a graduate opening in two years. Are you willing to try this?"

"Yes, Coach Faylor. **I know I can win.**"

Faylor shook his head at this expression of youthful invincibility. "Be careful what you say. It may come back to haunt you. The mermaid's head is smiling. Beware of the dragon's tail. Keep in mind that your goals must be in your heart and that a determined heart with great enthusiasm can overcome all obstacles.

"Call me next week. I'll contact the school today and get this started. Take this whistle." Coach Faylor took a new whistle out of his desk drawer and handed it to Little K. "When you return in two years we will talk about whether it has turned to gold or not. Good luck."

Little K took the whistle, trying to keep his fingers from trembling. His head was whirling with the insights that Coach Faylor had given him. He wanted time to write down his thoughts and process these new ideas, but most of it was swept aside by his overwhelming excitement about the opportunity he had just been given. He thought, *I'd sure like to have the golden whistle that coach Faylor wears around his neck. Maybe someday, maybe someday.* He felt incoherent as he tried to find words to thank Coach Faylor, and finally managed a few: "Thank you so much, sir. This means everything to me. **I know I can win.**"

"Are you sure you want to coach for the right reasons? Do you think you are prepared? You have been a great young man in our program. You have made me proud to be a coach."

Coach Faylor smiled, patted him on the shoulder and then gave him a back slap as he ushered the young man out of his office. He closed the door and returned to his oversized leather chair and sat down, thinking, *I wonder,* as he snapped his fingers.

CHAPTER 4
THE UPS AND DOWNS
OF COACHING

L ittle K's heart was racing and his head felt a little light; he had difficulty in keeping a smile off his face; a smile that was so wide that he knew he looked ridiculous. But he couldn't help it. He was headed for the arena for just about the most important moment in his life—the chance to become head coach for one of the greatest programs in the country.

He strode through the empty offices of the head coach's suite. It was late afternoon and everyone had gone home for the day. When Faylor's secretary had phoned to arrange the appointment, she had told him to just knock directly on the door of the coach's private office. Little K knocked on and then opened the door of Coach Faylor's office. He saw that the older coach was on the phone but before he could close the door again, Faylor motioned to him to sit down and mouthed, "I'll just be a minute. It's Coach Wooden."

Wow! thought Little K. *It's Coach Wooden!*

Little K settled into the big leather chair and looked around. The magnificent office seemed a little tired. As Little K looked at his boss and mentor, he could see a weariness about him that he'd never noticed before. He could see the coach was tired, but he could also see the spirit that had made him such a great teacher and coach.

Little K's thoughts drifted back five years to the other significant time that he had sat in this chair. The circumstances were completely different. He had brought his whistle back thinking he might never coach again. He had learned the biggest lesson of his life—winning wasn't as important as he'd thought before he started coaching. He had also earned a big dose of humility.

In his reverie he remembered saying, "Coach, I brought you my whistle. I really wished at times I was back cleaning the floor for you. By now I'm sure you've heard about my failure."

Little K smiled ruefully to himself as he recalled how he had almost thrown himself into the guest chair and slumped into the seat after placing his whistle on Coach Faylor's wide mahogany desk. It was the only time he'd ever been indifferent about how he presented himself to his respected mentor, but he had been so dejected that he simply hadn't cared.

Little K drifted further into his memories, remembering that Faylor had raised his eyebrows as the young coach sat down, but said nothing. That silence had loosened Little K's tongue completely, and his outburst had continued, almost without a breath, for the next ten minutes.

"Coach, I couldn't believe it when I got to the school and learned that you had coached there early in your career. I had no idea! No wonder you were able to get that position for me, especially knowing that you won a state championship there in your second year. But after being there for two years myself, I'm amazed that a state championship could ever have been possible at that school. It's funny how I just can't comprehend that. What a great accomplishment—and I couldn't even have a winning season.

"I've asked myself often why the people in the town seemed to oppose everything that I wanted to do. It's as though they didn't even want to win. Maybe I'm not cut out to be a head coach. I can hear people laughing at me right now. But I do know that I tried hard and gave it my best effort."

"Do you think you were too concerned with winning?" Coach Faylor queried. "I am sure I was," replied Little K.

"I didn't have any doubts when I arrived at the school, but they soon questioned everything I tried and doubts started to creep into my mind. No wonder they have lost so much; they are so negative. I was so confident --probably too much; even a little cocky—and now realize that I had not paid the price to even dream of greatness. It was a tough time, but in the course of those two years I learned a great deal. I learned that winning isn't the most important thing.

"I learned it wasn't as easy as I thought it would be. The players were great, the administration was defensive and seemed to be afraid of the parents. They sided with the parents on every issue. The parents were good if their son was playing, so we had five sets of happy parents. Five were lukewarm, depending on how much playing time their kid got, and two were convinced I was screwing their young darling.

"Do I sound a little bitter? Not as much as I was. I do know that I'm much more aware now.

"The fans seemed to turn on me after the first loss. They yelled that I was too young, not ready to coach, that I had no discipline and that slow-down style went out years ago. At the end of the final game, they chanted, 'Grow up somewhere else!'

Little K's thoughts continued to race. "Perhaps I should have been an assistant for a couple of years. I felt horrible. But I stood my ground. I remembered your words; they echoed in my ears: 'I expect you to have class.' So I held my head up, remained respectful while acknowledging people's criticisms, and kept my integrity.

"But my ego had control. I really thought I knew it all. I told people how good I would be and I really expected to be good. My ego was bigger than a mountain and I was reminded of one of the Aesop's Fables you taught in your 'Principles' class: There was a large volcanic mountain and for weeks it bellowed and thundered and finally the mountain cracked and split in two all the way to the bottom. A small mouse appeared and squeaked. No explosion, no lava, no thunderous sound. The lesson was 'Much outcry, little outcome.' That was me! But, boy, did I learn a great lesson in life and it strengthened my resolve. I no longer needed to win, I just needed to become the best I could be. Much outcry, little outcome, but I always believed the best was yet to come.

"The criticisms really began the first year when I started a freshman, who was our best player, but whose dad was president of the school board. Everyone accused me of brown-nosing and sucking up. The truth is, his dad wanted to coach and was a pain in the butt, because he thought he knew more about coaching than anyone. He became angry and created more problems when I told him I didn't want his help. It was a tough place to be in your first coaching assignment. Of course I realize that now. But I was so full of myself that I could not see it at the time.

"I started his son because he was a great kid and going to be a great player. I knew right away he was the real deal. Yes, he was skinny—5'7", 125 pounds—he was thin but wiry, really strong and really quick; a good ball handler and the most determined young man I have ever been around.

"The first time I saw Jay he was in the gym working on the daily dozen dribbling drills that the coach from the previous year had given him. He also shot 200 shots every day and lifted with the football team. The football coach had told me he could bench 175 pounds, which was fifty pounds more than his weight. He had an engaging smile and a great attitude. The word on the street was correct—he was an amazing basketball player.

"The rub was that his father was very dominant and pushy. He had tried to play basketball in college, got cut, and still held a grudge against all coaches.

"The only thing that got me through that first year was imagining the faces of the players, the parents and the townspeople as they laughed at me for failing—and I kept working harder. It was difficult for me to keep getting beat and keep thinking that someday I would be a great college coach. What a joke! I really thought I could win. The truth is that I had no idea what it took. But going one and nineteen that first year sure opened my eyes. It humbled me, and yet it only increased my resolve to be a better coach. I know now I should have reached out for more help.

"I faced despair and doubt and defeat and carried on. My ego took quite a beating. I have never smoked or drunk, but in the despair and loneliness of losing I certainly thought that getting drunk would help me forget.

"Mr. Bell, our custodian, ran me out of the gym several nights at midnight after I'd been shooting fouls for a couple of hours—that was the only thing that seemed to release the pressure! I was hurt and lonely. The first year was a long one, but it was one of the great challenges of my life and one of the great learning experiences. Finally the revelation hit me: I needed to ask people for help and share my feelings with others. You know I leaned on you much more the second year.

"You were right. All I worried about was winning, but I realize now that I wasn't ready to win.

"After that first year fiasco I discovered that the only real handicap we have in life is a bad attitude, with an assist from being cocky. I finally began to really understand what you meant, Coach Faylor, about Solution-Based Basketball. I realized that I needed to take my own problems and solve this.

"So I created a disciplined learning and development program for myself that started in the summer and continued into the school year with adjustments for my teaching and coaching schedule. I started a summer camp. I studied video. I worked harder than ever with the players individually, and I talked with several high school coaching legends and college coaches. I decided to go with the Princeton Offense because it seemed to fit our personnel: a big 6'5" post man who could really pass it and shoot the three; and hard-nosed tough kids who could shoot the three and cut hard to the basket.

"It seemed that the players were coming around. I worked with them in the classroom and spent time with them socially, trying to instill the class that you have given me. I was really proud when two of the seniors from my first-year team went to college to continue their education and become better young men—to become true student-athletes. One hoped to become a lawyer; he was a great student and leader for us. The other said he wanted to become a coach like me. That made me feel so proud.

"It didn't take long after the first loss of the season my second year to yank me back to reality. No wonder people call this school a graveyard for coaches. The fans seemed upset that I started four seniors and one sophomore, because we had one senior who did not play.

"The players kept working and I saw real flashes of improvement. I was excited about watching them grow as players, but more importantly, as young men. My little freshman, Jay, was growing up now as a sophomore, and I knew he could become an all-state player someday. Even his dad smiled at me after we won three in a row.

"One of my biggest challenges came with the senior who was on the bench and was one of the great young men I have ever been around. Myron had a four point academic record, he scored thirty-two on the ACT (which is unheard of in this community), he was president of his senior class and he was accepted early admission with a full academic scholarship to Harvard. He also happened to be the only African-American on the team. His dad had been an all-state football player, but hurt his knee; he was a custodian at the school but also was the baritone soloist in the school's annual *Messiah* performance; his mom was an English teacher at the school. The senior worked hard and was good for the team. The problem was that he just wasn't a very good basketball player. He came in and wanted to quit to spend more time on academics and on weight lifting. But I thought he could help us because of his attitude and desire, so I told him that if he stayed and worked hard I would start him the last game. He seemed excited about that and as the year unfolded he was a great leader for our team.

"You know the rest of the story. We were nine and 10 and had a chance to go .500 for the season. It was our last game. I remembered my promise to start him, even though I wanted to win in the worst way. I had given my word and decided that would be the best thing to do. I was starting him in place of the sophomore who said he understood, but I guess his father didn't. He stormed into my office the day before the game and screamed, 'We're not running an intramural program. Not starting my son is ridiculous.' He threatened to not let his son play at all if he didn't start."

Little K's thoughts digressed for a moment. "It didn't help that his daughter, Jamie, was a beautiful young cheerleader who often stopped in my office to talk. I told her she was not allowed in my office unaccompanied. I told her, 'You know that people talk.' She just smiled and said that she understood; from then on she brought one of the other cheerleaders, Hoopsie, Carolyn or Batesie, with her.

"Coach Faylor, you told me once that coaching is more about all the other things than just about the game. When I went to put the sophomore in during the game, he said that his dad told him not to play. He said that he loved me and the program, but he had to do what his dad told him. We played without him and lost the game. His dad accosted me after the game and said I was through. I'm not sure I did the best thing, but I did what I thought was right. That's what you taught me. Handle the tough times with class!

"I started a roundball boosters group headed by a couple of men who remembered when you coached there. Do the names Gary Bradley and Bill Geyer ring a bell? I wish I had more fans like them. I had the team do fundraisers for cancer research, got parents involved in helping with academics, got our counselors to write to colleges about our players and had our players coach the fifth and sixth graders. But no matter what I did, it didn't seem to be enough. I tried to be the best teacher I could be; teaching both math and biology was a great challenge, but I loved to teach.

"Still, the rumor mill was flying. Many people thought I was too young, that I flirted with the cheerleaders and that the offense I chose was absolutely the worst. They thought that the Princeton was nothing but slow-down crap that ruined the players' chances for a scholarship. Parents can be wonderful and they can be, well, I'm sure you know." Faylor just smiled.

"In spite of it all, I tried to show class in every situation. I could always hear your voice in my head: 'the one thing I will ask of you is to have class.'

"I have come to give back my whistle today. Maybe I'm not cut out to coach." Kichael's flood of words finally stopped. He slumped even further down in his seat and stared at his hands. In utter mortification he felt tears running down his cheeks and was unable to control them, nor the accompanying sniffle.

Faylor's words broke through Kichael's emotional fog. "You've had quite an exciting two years," said the older man.

"You even think that you have failed. In my eyes you have not failed, but have succeeded beyond my expectations."

Kichael's tears abruptly stopped and he looked at his coach in astonishment. Faylor smiled and continued,

"You loved your teaching.

You loved your players.

You handled adversity.

You never complained.

You did the right things.

You did things to help others.

You have learned a great deal.

You have been humbled.

Your whistle, though not gold, is starting to glisten.

There is a definite sparkle in the lower left corner."

Faylor handed the whistle back to Little K and motioned for him to return it to his pocket. Slowly, Kichael did so.

The older coach continued, "The hard work, the desire to do the best you could, the toughness in difficult situations, the perseverance, the belief that it will get better, pays off."

CHAPTER 5
THE BEGINNING OF
A GOLDEN FUTURE

Little K had been so lost in memory that he had forgotten where he was. Coach Faylor's voice saying, "Thanks for coming in this afternoon" jolted him back to the present and his new opportunity.

Faylor said, "You look like you've been daydreaming," and Little K responded, "That's an understatement. Were you really on the phone with John Wooden?"

Faylor replied, "Yes. John and I have been really close over the years. He even had his own set of golden nuggets. His Pyramid of Success is really unbelievable. He developed his own Big Word Offense. I'm sure you have read it, but have you engaged it in your life? We were reminiscing just now, and he told me how he had never seen Lew Alcindor play before he recruited Lew for UCLA. My, how quickly and how enormously times have changed."

Little K said, "And here I am recruiting an eighth grader who I've already seen five times. It's hard for me to imagine what things will be like in five years, much less fifty." "Well, you just might be in a great position to influence those changes, Little K. It 's been five years since you were given the ten golden nuggets to study. Are you ready to become a head coach?" As always, Coach Faylor went straight to the point.

"I'm not sure that anyone is ever ready," replied Little K, showing his increased maturity, "but I'm much more prepared than I was for my first job. You're giving me a great chance and a team that should be great. What a challenge for me not to screw it up.

"But ... I think I'm as ready as I can be. I'm excited and scared at the same time. I'll work hard to make you proud. I will always try to have class and I'll always strive to continue to earn the golden whistle every day that I coach. Thank you for this honor."

Coach Faylor looked at him for several moments. "It will only be an honor if you work every day of your life to become the best coach you can be. That's the honor. Continue to make me proud of you."

The veteran coach broke the awkward silence that followed by saying, "Let's take a look at the nuggets that are on the computer." Little K interjected, "Before you do that, I wanted you to know that Jamie, the cheerleader who graduated five years ago, just finished her master's in counseling and has accepted my proposal of marriage." Kichael pulled his whistle out of his pocket, blew it loudly in celebration of his announcement, grinned widely and put it back in his pocket. This made Coach Faylor laugh out loud. "Wow! Congratulations. I guess I should have figured out that was coming."

As Faylor plugged the flash drive into the computer, Little K continued, "And there's more news. My former player Myron just graduated from Harvard this week and has been named a Rhodes Scholar candidate. And that star player, Jay, the son of the school board president, is doing a great job with the Buckeyes after leading my old team to its second state championship. His dad has mellowed a lot and told me that he and Jay both gave me a lot of credit for this."

"So now do you finally believe me when I told you that your two years at the school were actually a success, not a failure?" asked Faylor, raising his eyebrows.

"You're always right, Coach," replied Little K with a wink.

"Good answer!" The two coaches grinned at each other in perfect understanding.

"OK, let's get to work," continued Faylor. "I will ask only two things of you. First, apply the nuggets and share them with anyone who asks. I want you to do this through an annual clinic that will generate money for Coaches vs. Cancer. Second, use the principles of Solution-Based Basketball to always strive to become a better coach, teacher and family man."

Little K smiled and said, "Thanks, Coach. These past five years have prepared me, but only God knows if I'm ready." Little K snapped his fingers, echoing his mentor's trademark action. "Let's look at the flash drive. Coach, what did you think of my 'From the Locker Room' quotes that I based on your 'From the Office' and Coach Aupp's 'From the Class-room' quotes that are already in the notebooks?"

"I like them very much," replied Faylor. "Remember, the essence of Solution-Based Basketball and the truth about earning a golden whistle is to study and learn from the masters and make that information your own, as you have done for the past five years. You academic types would call that 'infusion,'" he added with a sly grin.

"The reason I'm smiling is that I remember the first time I went to Las Vegas and saw all those Elvis Presley imitators—you know I'm big on Elvis. They were good, some were really good, but they couldn't be really great because they reproduced exactly what Elvis did and did not add anything new of their own. As you know, everything I do has basketball hooked to it. It's the same with coaching. To find real greatness you must take from great people and coaches and then use that and adapt it to become your own unique person. You can't just impersonate. You can't coach like me."

"Coach, that is such a tremendous analogy. If you don't mind, I'm going to steal it and use it to help explain Solution-Based Basketball to my assistants," smiled Little K.

"Once again, you get an A," joked Faylor. "I've already added 'From the Locker Room' to the nuggets on the computer files, along with some letters and documents from Coach Aupp, myself, and even some that you wrote. I think you'll find that these new sections will give you an even deeper understanding of the nuggets contained in those old notebooks you've been studying. Now, let's take a look, because this will become the basis for your coaching on the floor and off. I hope it will be a golden journey as mine has been." He snapped his fingers and both of them understood. They turned to the computer screen and began to read.

Ninety minutes later Little K emerged from the arena, his head filled with ideas from their review of the nuggets. He felt like he was walking on air. He headed toward his favorite coffee shop that was just off campus, ordered his favorite brew, sat down and pulled out his laptop. He wanted to look again at those nuggets that he'd studied for the past five years. He wondered what he might add during his years as a head coach and thought about how these nuggets had guided him so well over the past five years. Thoughts raced through his mind about the history of basketball that led to these nuggets and marveled that he was sitting there today, in this coffee shop, with a game that had gone from rags and peach baskets to the world of basketball on a flash drive. He was excited to look again at the new sections and even go through the nuggets again. As the document opened on the screen, he saw the bold words, "Coach Aupp's personal note to Coach Faylor" and began reading.

COACH AUPP'S PERSONAL NOTE TO COACH FAYLOR

Dear Coach Faylor,

Since we talked last week at the NCAA convention and I gave you the ten Golden Nuggets that helped shape my coaching career, I thought it might be beneficial to give you some more guidance.

Acquiring and keeping your own Golden Whistle will be a challenge you will need to accept every year that you coach. The challenge is a simple twofold process.

1. *Take your coaching to a level that your players deserve.*

You must never lose sight of the value of constantly learning and growing with the game. I saw it change in my forty years and you will see it change even faster in your career.

I smile when I think of the many coaches who attempted to acquire greatness in coaching without putting in the time and effort. You and I realize it takes a great deal of time and effort, constant learning and dedication to stay on top year after year. There are no shortcuts.

Study the nuggets. Develop your own process and style. Be yourself, but always listen to others.

2. *Become the best you can and be able to teach what you know to your players.*

A lot of coaches have failed because they became overwhelmed and complained of not having enough time. The secret to a solution-based basketball process is developing purposeful preparation for every day you coach. In addition, you must keep that preparation in perspective for how you handle the players, your family and all the people involved. We've discussed that before.

Your process and your preparation will help define you. Be sure and think about the following as you prepare for the future.

I usually begin practice with a quote, as many coaches do. What I also like to do is give the players a 'word for the day' that they can live in practice and in life: words like 'relationships,' 'energy,' 'health,' 'overload,' 'hours.' This is what I affectionately call the Big Word Offense. This is so important to my work that it has claimed a place as a Golden Nugget—the very first one.

INTRODUCTION TO THE BIG WORD OFFENSE

1. **Relationships.** How will you manage your players' parents, your family, other coaches, officials, administrators, fans, press and alumni? Be prepared so you don't respond in an emotional way, but rather be prepared for positive and negative reactions. Ask the players about their relationships, particularly with parents and teachers.

2. **Energy.** You are young and have an abundance of energy today, but you must know your limits mentally, physically and emotionally. Be aware of burnout, frustration, anger and disappointments. These sap your energy and cause you to make emotional decisions. Know your energy state and take precautions to protect it. Talk to the players about energy sappers.

3. **Health.** Of course your health is tied to your energy, but you must not take the game so seriously that it takes a toll on your body. Find an escape, something that gives you a sense of joy and recreation that will allow you to balance your life. I tell you this as a friend: watch what you eat and drink. Watch how much time you spend worrying or complaining. Take care of your health. The players' diets

are often very bad. Help them eat better. You, too, need to eat better and this will also help the players.

4. **Overload** combines the preceding elements. It keeps you from having perspective. Overload comes from too much practice, spending too long in video review sessions, holding too many meetings and spending too little time at home or with your family. Too much time can be as dangerous as too little time. The players can get overloaded from staying up too late and even just fooling around.

5. **Hours.** Are you meeting to meet or are you meeting to accomplish specific goals? Do you work late and arrive early? Do you take vacations with your family but are there in body and not in heart and spirit? Are you always somewhere else? Remember, time is currency. Spend it wisely. The players must watch out for time wasters.

Most coaches know the X's and O's and the fundamentals of the game. It's the other things that often do them in. Prepare for the unexpected, react in a manner that you have already prepared for. This is a great challenge.

I will watch you with great interest. Please never hesitate to give this "old" coach a call if you need me.

Drink deeply from the Golden Nuggets,
Coach Aupp

COACH FAYLOR'S REPLY TO COACH AUPP

Dear Coach Aupp,

Thanks for your kind words and encouragement. You have always been one of my coaching idols, and to have you as a mentor means more to me than I can ever express.

I realized early that coaching is a lot more than X's and O's, even though those are very important. It's also about the concomitant aspects of coaching. I have already been pondering the five factors—the Big Words–you gave me that relate to being a great coach. I've thought deeply about relationships, energy, health, overload and hours, and have benefited from the insights I have gained. For example, I've really been paying attention to my relationship with my wife and family and realize just how easy it is to lose sight of their needs.

Thinking deeply about these has also helped me develop my own solution-based basketball process. My first attempt at a purposeful process follows:

1. Ask a lot of questions.

2. Gather information.

3. Put action steps into place.

4. Try various options.

5. Always ask, "What is my purpose?" "Does it lead toward long-term improvement?"

As I start to develop my own style, my own program, my own philosophy, my own learning process, I need to apply these to all aspects of the game. For example, what if my team is having trouble with turnovers? I must go deep and wide into all aspects of the game.

1. **Ask a lot of questions.**

   - Who is turning it over? Are they experienced? Are they forcing things?

   - Why are they turning it over? Bad passes? Dribbling mistakes? Lack of concentration? Other team is quicker?

   - What can I do to help reduce the turnovers? What is my reaction as a coach when turnovers occur? Am I causing the players to fear making a mistake? Do I allow degrees of freedom? For example, a turnover made with great effort might be easier to tolerate. Do I spend too much time on turnovers with the players, which can also make them too cautious?

   - Where and when are the turnovers occurring? Early in the game? Late in the game? Certain places on the floor, e.g. post feeds? Late in the game when the pressure is on?

2. **Gather information.**

   - Review game tapes, films and statistics.

   - Chart all turnovers: Forced or unforced? Errors of commission or errors of omission?

3. **Put action steps in place.**

   - Share the charts with the players. Explain them and answer all questions.

   - Explain in a positive and firm manner where the turnovers occurred and how you and the players are going to correct them.

- The Big Word Offense can mean lots of different things. I can use negative-sounding words in non-emotional situations to reinforce the positive. In this case, I can ask the players, "Do you fear making turnovers?" and then have a conversation about fear. I can ask them, "Do you feel like you fail when you make a turnover?" and explain how the only failure is in not trying to improve or get better.

- There is a delicate balance in building confidence and destroying it. You must be aware of this when coaching turnover correction and in most other areas of coaching as well.

- Always discuss the who, what, where, why, when and how of each turnover.

- Have specific drills to work on to minimize the turnovers. These might be for physical correction, e.g. work on daily dozen dribbling drills; or for mental correction, e.g. don't get caught in the quick trap area.

- Be firm. Be fair. Be consistent.

4. **Try out various options to help correct the turnovers.**

- Have everyone run. The old coach is still with me. But this is a great place to talk about teamwork and toughness.

- Have only the players who made unforced errors run.

- Have players explain to the team and coaches.

- Talk about specific situations where certain turnovers are likely to occur. This helps increase awareness in the players.

- Work on technique, choices and adaptation to

improve turnover ratio. Explaining these three words is part of the Big Word Offense.

- Don't let players react physically or verbally—or pout—about a turnover in practice or in games. Body awareness must be addressed.

- Sometimes I need to get players' attention. But most of the time I need to be concerned with reactions and attitudes.

5. **What is the purpose of what I do? Does it lead toward long-term improvement?**

- I must be careful not to fall for quick but temporary band-aid fixes.

- My reaction to turnovers, e.g. taking a player out and reprimanding* him in front of other players, fans and parents may get his attention and may sometimes work, but I've got to create an atmosphere where the players are not afraid to make mistakes and are always wanting to get better if they do.

This process that I've followed with turnovers can be repeated with shot selection, with defensive play, with press offense, with any phase of the game, so that I continue to become a better coach and do not coach from a position of being surprised. I want to coach my players to be change-ready.

This process will evolve and grow and become better as I gain more insights into each player and more insights into the game.

Yours in Solution-Based Basketball,
Coach Faylor

*Another good Big Word Offense discussion

COACH FAYLOR'S PERSONAL NOTE TO LITTLE K

Dear Little K,

The great Coach Aupp gave these Golden Nuggets to me. I studied them and made them my own. I added a few things that seemed to fit my program and the changes in the game, called "From the Classroom." Of course, he gave me permission to do so. I've also included our exchange of letters to help you gain perspective.

You need to develop your own process and your own philosophy for learning the nuggets. It will not be easy, but what a great challenge for you as a coach.

You will never stop earning your Golden Whistle as long as you coach. Enjoy the journey.

Coach Faylor

LITTLE K'S REPLY TO COACH FAYLOR

Dear Coach Faylor,

I have read and re-read Coach Aupp's process and have studied your process and made my first feeble attempt at my own adaptation.

You told me I could steal from you, so I did. But you also cautioned me to make it my own, which I am doing.

Following my own process will give me great insights into all aspects of the game and will help me develop my own philosophy. I realize this will be a 'work in progress' for the rest of my coaching career. Thanks for going into such depth on the turnovers. It really helps me be aware of how much I need to learn.

Thanks for trusting me with the Golden Nuggets. I will make you proud! Here is my humble attempt at my own learning process.

1. **Identify and prioritize each specific area I want to grow in each year.**

I will try to study a new area of basketball each year. For example, I studied shooting last year and the match-up zone this year. I used your process, asked a lot of questions and am starting to use my own.

I have even taken a subject outside of basketball to grow in along with a basketball topic. I have only done this for a couple of years, but I studied piano and automotive repair. I plan to study classical music, how to add a room in the basement, stars and constellations, poetry and learn about the trees on campus. I have a blog and website. Please sign up if you want.

2. **Set goals and objectives.**

This is about purposeful preparation. It is about deep

learning. It is about disciplining myself to continue to grow as a coach and as a person.

I am making these goals fit my style, my level, and hopefully will apply these to my own program. I will be sure to include players and assistant coaches to help me in this.

3. Gather information.

Today the use of the computer is essential. But I also read books and magazines, talk with other coaches, attend clinics, watch others practice and watch games on TV. Having a mentor like you to turn to really helps.

Coaches have access to a lot of information today, but need help to put this knowledge into proper perspective. I hope coaches would seek proper training courses, attend clinics, be lucky enough to find a mentor. Fortunately, more and more of this is available virtually as well as in the traditional live venues. I know that one or two coaches have given live interactive coaching webinars. This could be the wave of the future.

4. Take the information and put it into teachable steps.

I have put the information into levels of complexity and sequenced my teaching of the material so that it becomes simple to learn and to teach. I want to make sure it fits my own program and my players. I always remember that you told me, "It's not as much what you know as what you can teach." I also have a framed copy of the Jesse Feiring Williams quote, "Education of the physical or **through** the physical" on my desk.

5. Gather other coaches for a peer-based seminar or clinic.

I did this for the first time this summer. It was tremendous. Hopefully we will do it every year. The topic was the 'match-up' defense because that was my basketball topic of the year. I asked the others to bring questions and thoughts. I challenged them to study the topic before they arrived. I presented my thoughts, my questions and my challenges; then I listened and made adjustments. Afterwards, I synthesized everyone's thoughts and shared the results with all the participants. This is a tremendous learning venue.

6. **Test my results in practice.**

Now I need to see if it all works. Does it fit my players? For example, a control offense for players who like to run might be a tough sell. I know that I can't implement big changes until I am sure that the players and I are on the same page.

7. **Get up to date with technology.**

Technology is not only a fact of life in sports today, it may very well be the driving factor in the future of sports—outside of people skills, of course! So I'll continue to keep up. When I got together with the other coaches, we talked about how even older coaches must find a way to be "with it." We recently purchased the bluetooth-enabled 94Fifty ball to help measure our players' skills. This is scary, but it's our reality.

8. **I'll repeat the process for everything I learn for as long as I coach.**

Each coach must develop his or her own style, solutions, purposeful preparations and philosophy. What did you call this? Infusion!

What a challenge! I accept!

Little K

P.S. I have followed your practice of defining a word for the day. Not just the big, hard words like 'reminiscence,' but the big, important words like 'love,' 'caring,' and 'kindness.'

I have never started a class without the word for the day. The Big Word Offense has really helped me.

You talked about 'reminiscence' before practice one day. I looked it up later to get more insight. What a great word. I've sent you an email with the definition, as I know you are becoming a techie! I love the Big Word Offense!

INTRODUCTION TO THE TEN NUGGETS

by Coach Aupp

Although the coach's job is about X and O's, skill development and fundamental improvement, it seems that other areas usually dominate his time and attention.

Recruiting at the college level, promotion, fundraising, public relationships, salesmanship, booster meetings, player problems and concerns, officials, rule changes, parents and fans all take valuable time and energy. These areas can be very distracting and can even be a larger cause of failure than a coach's knowledge of the game. It is my hope that the Golden Nuggets will help a coach in these areas.

The wise coach should study a variety of coaches and look for ideas from each of them. He can then incorporate bits and pieces of each into his own philosophy and develop his own style and process. Through this exploration he should pick or choose principles that fit his particular situation and players. Develop your own thoughts, but be prepared to adjust. This is a great way to start running the Big Word Offense.

RELATIONSHIPS

The coach needs to be a person of high standards. He is being entrusted with boys and girls who are growing into men and women. This is a critical time. This refers to all levels—seventh grade to college kids will be affected by the coach. The coach as a guidance counselor is a good analogy, but how many coaches have studied or are trained in counseling? You need to be aware of the impact and influence you have on your players, not just as an athlete but in life.

TEACHING

Each coach must develop his own theories regarding how to teach the game and reach the players. Teach and reach. Some will have a definite plan and then they have the players adjust to that plan. Others will adjust their style to fit the players. Some change from season to season and even from game to game. Some spend most of their practice time scrimmaging or in 5 on 5 play. Some spend most of their time devoted to half-court drills or group and individual fundamental drills. Some work mostly individual drills—1 on 1 and 2 on 2. Some have a meticulous timetable and plan.

What will be **your** style and purpose?

THOUGHTS ON LEARNING

To get the best results in the shortest time with your players, it helps to know some laws of learning and teaching methods. These will also help you as a coach in your own learning process.

1. See the whole, then teach the part. This is a principle of Gestalt psychology.

2. Intrinsic motivation—The desire to learn and the desire to win must come from each person; it can't be imposed from the outside. The teacher/coach's task is to find ways to trigger intrinsic motivation, both in himself and in his players.

3. Repetition—Done properly in short time segments and repeated often.

4. Plateaus—Maturation when losing. Should you practice more or less?

5. Practices—Amount, type, strenuousness, mental aspects. Vary your practices based on your situation, your circumstances and the stage of the season.

6. Use various teaching devices and extrinsic motivational methods to enhance the intrinsic aspects.

COACHING STRATEGY

You'll need to build in this and develop your own so you're as proactive as possible. Here are a few to get you started.

1. Make opponents do things they don't want to do.

2. Substitute for tactical purposes, not to punish a player for an error.

3. Take time outs for tactical reasons only.

4. Have 'passing' tactics and 'being passed' tactics.

5. Fast break utilization

6. Ball control and freeze tactics

7. Late game situations

8. Defensive adjustments

9. Defense to stop the offensive strengths of the opponents.

Are you ready to coach all these areas? There are many more that you can create and make your own. Start your own list today.

INVISIBLE VISION

Most coaches learn fundamentals, rules, offenses and defenses, but never learn about the caustic, volatile and negative environment that often exists in the high-pressure world of basketball. The game can bring out the worst in people, who react and respond during game pressures in ways that they would never dream of behaving in other circumstances.

Knowledge of coaching and of the game doesn't guarantee success in the profession of basketball coaching. The real art is in putting it all together. You must refine, tweak and fit everything into your own style. Add a little here, subtract a little there and make it your own. Each coach must have his own style of success.

Warning!

Do not read these nuggets unless you are a coach who is hungry to become the best you can be.

STEPS TO GOLD

Process of Learning

by Little K

You should not read this book, you should engage it. Before you begin, ask yourself, "Why am I reading this book? What takeaways do I want to acquire?"

Step 1.

    A. The very first step is in choosing to read this book. Read it through entirely one time. Let it sink in. Think about it. Then re-read it, underlining points and writing notes in the margin to reinforce concepts that apply to you and your own set of circumstances and your own situation.

    B. Take time to go back and outline your thoughts by hand in a notebook. Writing in longhand helps to reinforce the learning of concepts. You can then type them. I'm a computer user, but I still take notes by hand and then transfer them to my computer to keep.

After the first read, you should start feeling some of your own thoughts creeping in.

This first step will propel you on your path. From now on, treat every book you read in the same manner. This is **purposeful preparation.** Make it part of your development as a coach for the rest of your career.

There is no preparation, no process, that can guarantee that you will be a great coach and earn your golden whistle. But in order to even get yourself in the running, you must, and can, point your steps in the right direction.

Step 2.

Re-read and engage each nugget and study it until it becomes a part of you and you make it a part of your coaching style.

Step 3.

Challenge those around you to read the book at the same time, then meet once a week to discuss the nuggets and how to apply them. I realize schedules are hectic. A Skype or Google hangout can work really well for this, but there's nothing like face-to-face get-togethers.

Are you ready to engage the challenge?

GOLDEN NUGGET NO. 1

The Big Word Offense: Our words reflect what is really in our heart.

Beyond

Go past where you have been;
reach out and become better.

Go beyond where you are today, every day.

Challenge yourself and your team
to always reach beyond where they are
and to become all they can become.

Welcome to the first nugget. As I have gotten older, I have been gathering thoughts on how I would do it better if I were starting over. These nuggets in general and the Big Word Offense in particular may help you develop as a coach and avoid the pitfalls and problems that all coaches are faced with. They existed in my day and are even more prevalent today. The nuggets involve a lot of things I would have done to keep getting better year after year.

If you were to ask most coaches what skills they look for in their players when selecting a team, you'd most likely get the following:

- He should be athletic, be able to run and jump and have good strength.

- He needs to have fundamental skills, particularly dribbling, passing and shooting on the move under pressure for the entire game.

- He would really help the team if he loved to play defense.

- If you add rebounding ability to all the other characteristics, you'd have a pretty complete player.

Most of us would agree these are important, but it's my belief that a lot is missing. The first thing that's missing is the Big Word Offense. Words like attitude, leadership, industriousness and communication, along with words like academic, intelligence, responsible, lifter, give and caring. I think you get the point.

The mental aspect certainly is as important or even more important as the physical aspects of basketball. Bob Knight used to say that the mental is to the physical as two is to one.

A good coach must be able to assess his players from the outside and from the inside. This is part of what I call Solution-Based Basketball and is the heart of coaching.

OUR WORDS REFLECT WHAT IS REALLY IN OUR HEART!

Don't just read the nuggets. Engage the nuggets. Well, go ahead and just read for now, but then later re-read it, let it sink in, let the thoughts become your thoughts so they fit your style and your program.

How would you describe your coaching? I want to know what **words** you would use. How will you describe your players? Are they big words—positive and uplifting—or small words—negative and degrading? Do you swear a lot? Do you demean the players? How do you speak to the parents? This is what I mean by the Big Word Offense.

You must watch your words diligently, for the words you speak have the capability of increasing positively the motivational levels of your players and conversely destroying their desire to play.

From the Locker Room—Little K

> Be quick to listen, deep when you look, slow to react and certain when you speak.
>
> —Bob Burkholder, Ohio State University assistant coach

From the Office—Coach Faylor

> "Someone has said that all living is just learning the meaning of words. That does not mean the long ten-syllable words we have to look up in the dictionary.
> The really great words to master are short ones: work, love, hope, joy, home, child, life, death."
>
> —Halford E. Luccock, author, minister, Harvard professor

Polishing the Nugget

After a very difficult loss, in my estimation we played **terrible.** We had twenty-seven turnovers, shot less than forty percent from the floor and twenty-three percent from the three point line. To remain consistent, we played **terrible** on defense and were out-rebounded.

I told our players after the game, "Let's talk about **terrible** tomorrow and you think about it tonight." I am certain they were thinking the worst.

At the beginning of every practice, we would have a short motivational and informational meeting to set the tone for practice. At the next day's meeting I asked the team how they thought we played. There was not a sound.

I said, "How about **terrible**? How were we handling the ball?" One player replied, "Terrible. We had twenty-seven turnovers, which was the most any team of yours has ever had."

I then asked him and the rest of the players how that made them feel. They all pretty much agreed: **Terrible.**

"How did we shoot the ball?" "Terrible."

"How did we rebound?" "Terrible."

"How did we play defense?" "Terrible."

"How was your effort?" One brave senior co-captain bravely blurted out, "Not great, but not terrible. It seemed the harder we tried, the worse we got."

"How did you react after the game? I saw players upset. I would say you were hurt, disappointed and embarrassed. No one said much on the way home.

"I noticed your reactions and felt lifted by your response. I felt hope in the fact you did not give up and that you might want to get better. And that's **not terrible.**

"Do you think we can get better and continue to work hard?"

In unison there was an enthusiastic "Yes!"

"Do you know what would be **terrible**? If we decided to give up and fight each other and the coach. We get to play this team again. We might not win. But it would be **terrible** if we didn't try to get better every day. Today I feel excited and that's not **terrible**—that's **terrific!** Let's go practice our butts off!"

P.S. We did win the next game against that team and it was **wonderful!** The Big Word Offense can turn **terrible** into **terrific.**

The Big Word Offense gives vision and direction. I challenge you to start:

1. Have a word for the day, every day. Define the simple words like hope, love and kindness. Look up words you don't know, study their meaning. Work them into your practice plan. Give them to the players every day. Don't tell me you don't have time. Start today and it will become a habit very quickly. Don't get **supercilious** on me! (To begin to **engage the nuggets**, look up the word 'supercilious' before you continue reading.)

2. Have a quote for the week—or even each day. Make sure it has meaning for you and the players. Work this into your practice.

3. Have a word for the year. You get to pick one that will inspire you throughout the year. One year my word was 'beyond' and that was the year that we needed to step it up and win an NCAA championship. Another year my word was 'allocate' because I wanted to spend more time with my wife and family.

4. Have a mantra for your life, for example: "The wind in the world blows toward good" or "Take the hardest day you've ever worked in your life and make that your average." Use this on every practice plan. Let the players decide, or perhaps you can give them a couple of choices.

This may seem a long way from X's and O's, but you must empower yourself so that you can empower the players. I want you to seek the higher way. It's what the great coaches have always sought.

The Big Word Offense gives vision and direction. It can be run as a pattern or freelance. I believe knowing and studying the meaning of the Big Word Offense will allow you to see more clearly what needs to be accomplished to become all you can become.

The great Ohio State football coach and professor Woody Hayes told me that he loved the book *Word Power Made Easy* and he taught words to his players on Sunday mornings. He was a great believer in the power of Big Words.

CAN YOU SEE WHAT PLAY TO RUN?

Vision—Is your vision clear for your basketball program? Can you make your players and your vision one vision? Visual awareness is seeing what needs to be done before the damage clouds your sight. I know that you can see clearly only when you become aware of your language and can articulate precisely where you want to go and what you want to do.

Just as we must be clear about what play to run, each player must know his responsibility on each play. They also must understand how the Big Word Offense runs. I've had players tell me they hate other players or they hate studying or they blame everything on someone else. A coach must be able to take those words, put them in perspective for the player and help the player become aware of the power, both good and bad, of their words. Can they *see* the value of the words they use?

What do you see when the following words appear? I'll give you the first one.

I see hate, you see _____love_____.

I see blame, you see _____.

I see doubt, you see _____.

I see trust, you see _____.

I see lower, you see _____.

I see terrible, you see_____.

I see horrible, you see _____.

I see character, you see _____.

I see patience, you see _____.

I see love, you see _____.

I can clearly see that all words carry in them the seeds of goodness or the seeds of hate. Developing the Big Word Offense and playing great defense on the Small Word Offense will give you confidence in coaching and how to handle people that you have not experienced before.

Our words reflect what is really in our heart.

I ask you, "What comes out of your mouth? Big words or small words? What is your vision? How good is your Big Word Offense?

WHERE, OH WHERE, HAVE THE X'S AND O'S GONE?

I have seen that most coaches do a good job with X's and O's. They love new plays. They study late game situations. They know the rules and regulations. But they seldom spend time pondering the impact of the words they say, talk, yell or scream to their players.

Our words reflect what is really in our heart.

You need to know words that inspire, words that lift, words that teach. I had the privilege of teaching as well as coaching and needed to know the words that allowed students to learn kinesiology. Words like 'sternocleidomastoideus', 'eccentric vs. concentric' (lengthening and shortening contractions.) These are not much value in coaching, although they could be helpful, but you must have a strong desire to learn the words of your subjects and of your coaching. You must believe in the power of your words to lift and motivate. I had a word for the day and a thought for the day in every class I taught.

From the Locker Room—Little K

> "Today we also need to know the digital
> words: tweet, RT, DM, LOL, link, follow,
> friend, hangout, app, ebook, cloud, download, etc."
>
> –Mike Crowley, 94Fifty CEO

SWEARING

In a court of law, when you put your hand on the Bible you say, "I swear to tell the truth, the whole truth and nothing but the truth."

On the court of basketball, you need to put your hand on the ball and swear to develop positive, uplifting language: "Dammit, I swear I will cut down on my swearing."

How would you describe your language? What sets you off? Poor play? Officials? Losing? Turnovers? All of these?

How would you describe your coaching? Tough? Hard? Old school? The words you use to describe yourself define you as a coach. How about caring, giving, understanding, consistent? Or reactive, hateful, cursing or short-tempered?

I often tell people, "My dad was a mechanic. He worked hard, he drank beer, he swore a lot. So when I get angry I revert back. It seems easy to blame my dad. It is a good excuse, even understandable, but it is not acceptable. I have never drunk in my life. However, I do still swear occasionally. So I really did make a choice.

I even got to the point where I had a manager keep track of my swear words during practice and the games. It was enlightening and made me aware that I needed to control my language. Awareness is a great word to use with the players and for yourself. I **can** get better. I **will** get better.

I discovered that I would swear when:

1. I was angry! At the players. At the officials. At my family. At the media. I needed to learn not to let situations that I could not control set me off. I asked myself, "How can I slow down my quick temper?" The key was by being aware of the situations **and** having a strong desire to improve.

From the Classroom—Coach Aupp

> *"He that is slow to anger is stronger than the mighty; he that ruleth his spirit than he that taketh a city."*
>
> –Proverbs 16:32

2. I reacted too quickly. I had a short fuse. I worked very hard at disciplining myself so I could then discipline the players. You can't say, "That's just the way I am." That's an excuse, not a reason. You **can** teach old coaches new words. You **can** lengthen your fuse.

Our words reflect what is in our heart.

Of course, you may still swear occasionally, but it should make you feel bad because it shows lack of class and character, two things you want as the basis for your program.

I challenge you to change and run the Big Word Offense.

DO YOU HAVE A SUBBING PLAN?

Coaches take time to know which players they will substitute; they have a subbing plan. In the same way you need to call some communication timeouts and sub Big Words in for the Small Words and Small Words (non-swearing) in for swearing.

Cut out the swear words as much as possible, but be aware that the Small Word Offense you run can be just as harmful. Words like:

Blame

Hopeless

Worthless

Terrible

Doubt

Fear

Worry

Awful

When you **blame** others or tell them they are **worthless** and **hopeless** as players, that they are **terrible** as a team and **doubt** if they will ever be any good, you put **fear** and **worry** as the things they think about most. What an **awful** way to coach.

The Small Word Offense creates a negative environment that often motivates out of fear. This can work in the short term, but never in the long run.

Our words reflect what is really in our hearts.

I contend that you must become aware of what you are now saying and try hard to maximize the words that lift and motivate. How do you react? What words do you speak? Do you fight anger with anger? How do you respond to criticism? Are you mad at officials even before the game begins? Awareness and willingness to change are a great combo.

Remember, basketball is a game. The players are kids or young adults. They need guidance and direction. I know that I have lost sight of that at times—I am still trying to run the Big Word Offense better.

From the Office—Coach Faylor

> "Mirror, mirror on the wall
> Can I improve my language at all?"
>
> –Page Moir, Roanoke College (Virginia) coach

TIME OUT FOR SUBSTITUTES

Love, get in for Anger.

Hope, replace Doubt. No, wait!

Vision, sub in for Doubt.

Hope, you get in for Can't.

Confidence, you stay in but talk to Worry.

Challenge, are you up to replacing Complacent?

OK. On the count of three, let's hear it: "What's in our hearts?"

Your words may not change the world. They may not help you win a lot more games, but they might make a difference to your team. If it makes a difference to one player, you have won the Golden Whistle.

To the Reader

Congratulations on reading the first nugget. Think about it. Let it become a part of you. Add your own thoughts. Start to develop your own process. The journey never ends.

1. Write down five takeaways from this nugget. Re-read as necessary.

2. What one theme dominates this first nugget?

3. What is the mantra?

4. What Big Word tips off the chapter?

GOLDEN NUGGET NO. 2

You Become Your Habits in Pressure Situations

Pressure

The coach needs to provide an atmosphere (enough pressure)
where good habits are developed on and off the floor.

"Repeat 4,999 times and then one more."
—*Coach Phog Allen, University of Kansas*

Welcome to the second nugget. Let's talk about habits. We all have good and bad ones. In coaching we often talk about discipline. It will take discipline—a lot of hard work and dedication—to maximize your positive habits. Habits are affected by pressure. The more pressure there is, the more our habits get exposed—the bad ones as well as the good ones.

Coaching is about handling pressure.

Note that I didn't tell you to get rid of your bad habits. I've found that when I focus on maximizing my positive traits, many of the less desirable ones fade into the background.

You must constantly question what you are doing. Habits sneak in the side doors and open windows and even blow through the cracks. Habits can be bad and block progress or good and lead to greatness. Do you open the door for bad habits to enter? Do you let them stay for just one night? Then a week and then a month and finally they are there to stay?

You may need help to weather-proof your house and you may need help to confront those bad habits and kick them out the front door.

Change them slowly and change them one at a time. Replace them with good ones. Little by little the bad one will lose its controlling power over you. Little by little the new one will take over and replace it.

The pressure will lessen as you learn to anticipate and handle difficult situations.

You want to coach? You'd better be prepared to handle the pressure.

A lot of great young men and women—bright, talented and highly motivated, have failed as coaches. Their failure is not due to lack of talent but due to lack of understanding. They do not understand the difficulties inherent in coaching, and they do not understand that they must develop habits that allow them to learn the golden nuggets of coaching success. They often avoid the real pressures until it's too late.

From this moment on, do it your way. Learn every day until learning becomes a habit.

Thus, the second nugget of Solution-Based Basketball is:

You become your habits in pressure situations.

You must form good habits and search for solutions. You must constantly learn about pressure and adjust to change. You must develop great habits of learning. Moreover, you must be able to teach these habits and adjust to individual players. This is a great challenge. How can you prepare?

Remember: You become your habits in pressure situations. You must make sure your habits are good ones.

Begin today!

From the Classroom—Coach Aupp

"Good habits formed in youth make all the difference."
—Aristotle

Develop good coaching habits and develop your own solution-based attitude and style:

1. See the problem clearly—ask a lot of questions.

2. Own the problem—make it your own. Be responsible.

3. Listen and observe—let the problem tell you what to do

4. Focus on being a part of the solution—Help the problem solve itself

5. Change purposefully and slowly.

The game is about understanding the players and teaching the players:

1. the fundamentals

2. how offenses and defenses work

3. rebounding

4. press offense and defense

5. specialties

The list goes on! It is also about knowing how to set up effective practices. It is about repetition, which will develop good habits of thinking and good habits of movement. These good habits will activate and help your team succeed in pressure situations.

Develop a deep knowledge of all aspects of the game. This will help take the pressure off.

In order to teach effectively, you must be able to look inside the players and motivate them to learn the game. The solution is to not only look into the hearts and minds of the players, but also to teach them as individuals and inspire them to blend together as a team.

You must do it your way. Understand that pressure is part of the game. Look for new ideas, sift through old ideas, pick the best and disregard the bad. Always look for the solutions that fit you best. This is what I mean by doing it your way.

Change your habits of learning the game. Don't drag misses into the next game. If you're letting the players shoot a lot in practice but letting them shoot it the wrong way, you're just reinforcing more bad shots.

Begin today. Accept the challenge to develop your personal and professional growth for yourself and for the sake of the players.

From the Locker Room—Little K

"500 shots = one good shot 500 times"

—Kevin Eastman, Los Angeles Clippers assistant coach

SEARCH FOR NUGGETS—THE SOONER THE BETTER

Search in places you've never been before. Explore and dig in new mines every day. Always dig with a purpose and passion. When not digging, sit down and pan for those nuggets.

Be careful of fool's gold—if you gather nuggets from another coach and then don't combine them with other nuggets and make them your own, then you've gained nothing.

Change how you learn the game. Dig deep to find your golden whistle. Develop great habits that will allow you to develop your own process, your own style.

If you keep looking, you keep finding those golden nuggets.

START TODAY

Today is the tip-off for the biggest game of your coaching career. Today, cast away old habits of doubt, despair, and discouragement and start a new game. You are changing the way you coach: now you'll coach the Solution-Based Basketball game. Lessen the negative pressure on yourself and that will lessen the pressure on the players.

Today, blow your whistle to start anew and turn that whistle into gold. Take a complete look at yourself; list your strengths and weaknesses and prepare yourself to become a great coach.

LOOK AT THE PAST

Sit at the feet of masters. Study old coaches, old games and learn the great history of our game. The history of the game will become a part of who you are. Without the work and effort of great coaches and players we would not be where we are today.

Stand on the shoulders of the giants in our game and make their thoughts your own. The game has changed—it is always changing—but your understanding of history will give you a strong foundation that will make it possible for you to successfully adjust as circumstances change. Good preparation makes it easier for you to find the best solutions.

It is essential to develop a deep knowledge of all aspects of the game.

Through studying the game you'll realize that even the giants had problems, that they faced tremendous pressure and challenges and found ways to handle them. Learn from them.

The fundamentals of the game endure but they evolve with time. What was successful yesterday may not work today. Study yesterday anyway.

FIND YOUR OWN STYLE

Remember this: You can and should learn a great deal from older coaches but you must adjust and apply the knowledge to your present situation. It's important to convert any lack of experience into an opportunity to learn. Experience can never be over-rated but be sure not to waste it talking about the good old days and living in the past.

Yes, it's good to look back to the two-hand set shot, the iron cross defenses, the key area, the center jump, the first jump shot. You need to look back and use that information to strengthen your fundamental knowledge of the game, but apply only what will work with your team today.

From the Office—Coach Faylor

> "Respect the past, learn from the
> past, but apply it to the now."
>
> —Don McKillip, Marysville, Ohio junior high
> coach and teacher

Work hard and work smart. Begin today to develop good habits that will help you become a great coach. Giving is one of the most important habits that you can develop: **Giving gets.** It is through giving that your coaching growth will take place.

Prepare to change. Constant learning will help you adjust to change. Do it your way. Keep in mind a mantra I used throughout my career: "Change with the times, but cling to unchanging principles."

SOLUTION-BASED BASKETBALL IS EVERYWHERE

I chose to be a coach and so did you. We chose coaching despite realizing the difficulties involved and the challenges that lay ahead. The practice of Solution-Based Basketball is the best way to prepare yourself for all circumstances and situations that will confront you. Coaching is full of great opportunities but also has many disappointments, heartbreak and despair. You must and will discover this for yourself and Solution-Based Basketball will help you successfully navigate the difficult times.

Can you become a great coach? If all the notes taken, all the books read about basketball, all the films, and coaches themselves who wanted to win but failed to prepare, were piled one on top of another they would fill the cavernous old Memorial Hall on the Kentucky campus. Yet it does not seem insurmountable.

Make this your mantra: I will not fail. I may lose some games, but as a coach I will not fail. I will accept the challenge.

The first thing you must understand is that there is no Harry Houdini, no prestidigitation, and no magic wand. Instead, you must be eager to constantly learn the game and adapt to change. You must embrace the pressures of coaching, knowing that they'll help you grow as a coach. The principles found in these nuggets can guide you toward your vision.

From the Office—Coach Faylor

"When you study, really study.
When you play, play hard."

—Bob Tucker, Marysville, Ohio high school coach and teacher

Coach Tucker gave me this saying when I left for college. It hangs above my desk to this day.

Many aspiring coaches with great potential fail to see the reality of coaching–the long hours, the work, the challenge. Many of them are not able to handle all the temptations surrounding coaching. The clinics become a time to party, to drink, to chase, instead of a time to grow and learn and apply the things they know to their own coaching. They feel entitled to win. They think that winning will take care of itself. They think that winning only happens on the game floor. Many coaches think that if they can win, even if they must cut corners a little, they will be happy. This idea will work sometimes, this may even work for a short time, but this will not work for a career. Observe, watch and control the pressure valve. Do it the right way.

From the Classroom—Coach Aupp

> "Nothing will bring you joy,
> peace of mind, and victory
> except the triumph of principles."
>
> —Ralph Waldo Emerson, "Essay on Self-Reliance"

COMMITMENT TO THE GAME

You must prepare yourself for the wisdom and principles found in these nuggets. They will guide you and keep you in a straight line to the basket.

The games, the practices, the seasons and your career will teach you a lot about yourself and basketball. But you cannot wait for experience alone in order to become a great coach. Experience could take a lifetime. No. Follow these nuggets and create your own learning process to earn your golden whistle. Balance excitement and patience, which will be a tremendous challenge. Do you accept the challenge?

Develop the habit of learning. Develop and follow your own learning process. I've always been a listener and learner. I read every book I could, I attended every possible clinic (in my younger days there weren't too many of either of these. This is changing rapidly.) I gathered information on notecards and created a good filing system and listened to the greatest minds of the game when they visited the Kansas campus.

From the Classroom—Coach Aupp

> "Habits provide a structure to our lives and
> keep us focused on what needs to be done."
>
> —George Klein, Ohio University assistant
> coach and teacher

HOW WILL YOU PREPARE?

Every game takes on a life of its own. You must be prepared for every possible situation and circumstance. In particular, you must be prepared for those late game situations in which good decisions can make such a difference and lead to big wins. What offense will you use? Should you play pressure or should you play a little softer and contain the defense? Even the time-outs need to be organized and prepared for in advance. This will help take the pressure off.

So much to do, so much to get ready for and so little time. Can one ever be fully prepared? Don't overwhelm yourself with that question. Focus on the small steps you can take right now that will make a difference. Start today, even if you have little knowledge or experience. Begin to build now. The journey looks impossible but you must take one dribble at a time and handle the pressure.

Demand good habits from your players and demand them of yourself. Whatever pressure coaches feel is felt by their players and all those around them. Preparation lessens pressure. Your good habits will even give you more time.

You become your habits in pressure situations.

Polishing the Nugget

When I was a young coach I had poor habits of going crazy, getting upset, yelling and swearing. Of course, I was really feeling the pressure to win and to keep my job.

Jack was a young player who wasn't getting to play as much as he wanted. He was a wonderful young man with great character. He was an outstanding student and also had the most engaging smile of anyone I have ever known.

And he was the only African-American player on the team. He was a joyful young man who was not living up to his own expectations as a player, nor to mine.

We were playing on the road in a tightly-contested, 'poorly' officiated game (poorly officiated in that I was angry at every call that went against us.) I needed Jack to go in for another player who was in foul trouble. He went in and immediately committed a dumb foul (or was it a 'bad' call?), turned the ball over and then took one of the worst shots I'd ever seen.

In my wrathful state I yelled, swore, took Jack out of the game and banished him to the end of the bench. We lost in overtime.

My anger was out of control and the pressure valve had exploded. I chased officials, yelled at the other coach, confronted some of the fans and headed to the locker room, completely failing to even think about how the players felt. I entered the locker room in my rage, yelling and screaming, and began throwing our sack lunches (which we were to eat on the way home) against the wall.

I looked up to see Jack coming toward me. And in my angered, out of control state of mind, I thought, "If he says anything to me . . ." Jack looked at me and said, "I'm sorry I didn't play well for you. I love you and I love playing with this team." The locker room went silent. The other players stopped feeling sorry for themselves and were watching Jack and me. I replied, "Damn, Jack, you've ruined a good rage." Then I smiled and said, "I'm sorry. Help me pick up the sack lunches and let's get home and win the next one."

I looked around at the other players and said, "It wasn't your fault we lost. It wasn't the officials' fault. The other team is good and they are tough and we can get better. It may well be my fault. I lost control and I pres-

> sured you. I will try to control myself better; that is part
> of the mental toughness we all need. I will get better!"
>
> This taught me a great lesson about habits and pres-
> sure. You can change, but in order to do that, you must
> first become aware. From that day on, I would occasionally
> get angry, but I got a lot better. Jack, let's go and get the
> next one!

FUNDAMENTAL PRINCIPLES

What will allow you to become a great coach and to win in
life and in the game? Engage these nuggets. They will help
you understand the fundamental principles in both basketball
and life and how to apply them. Failure will only occur if you
fail to develop your own learning process and to prepare as
you should.

The difference between good coaches and great coaches
lies in the development of their habits and how they handle pressure. Good habits are the key to unlocking all your
dreams of having great teams and winning championships.
Bad habits, however, can put a lid on the basket and stop you
from achieving your goals.

Pressure exposes all habits—good and bad. Be the captain
of your own pressure team. Before you demand good habits
from your players, demand them of yourself.

Develop good habits. Teach yourself first. By developing
skills and fundamentals as a coach, you will ignite the inner
spark in your players and motivate them to want to become
the best they can be. Embrace those tough pressure situations
that occur both on and off the floor. Be a role model and
mentor to your players. If you handle pressure situations with
class, so will your players.

From the Classroom—Coach Aupp

> "Good coaching may be defined as the
> development of character, personality, and
> habits of players, plus the teaching of
> fundamentals and team play."
>
> —Clair Bee, Long Island University coach and
> professor

Fundamentals remain essential to the game. Teach basic fundamentals to all your players. Teach yourself first.

At the same time, basketball is as much or more about the mental aspects as it is about the game or the fundamentals.

Increase your coaching expertise and also have good habits both mentally and physically.

Begin today to become better in all aspects of life, of teaching, and of coaching the game.

Winning brings the pressure of expectations. Losing brings the pressure of losing your job. Expect to feel the pressure, both good and bad. Awareness is the first step toward managing pressure.

I hope that this nugget helps you realize how important it is to change your habits of learning the game. You must pay the price in time and concentration. The rest of the nuggets will teach you more about Solution-Based Basketball, but you must first have the foundation of this nugget—the realization that habits can be changed for the better. Your goal must be to have each nugget become a part of your everyday behavior. The principle from each nugget must become a habit of living and of coaching and teaching.

HABITS STRENGTHEN CONVICTIONS

The key is consistency. Engage the nuggets every day. Do not deviate from them. They will become habit. No matter how much pressure you face, you will stay the course. Knowledge and preparation help you become more proactive in your coaching.

Habits are developed through constant repetition. Remember the words of the great Kansas coach, Phog Allen, from the beginning of this nugget: "Repeat 4,999 times …. then once more." The pressure is on to do just one more.

Practice what you preach.

Today, make a fresh start. Feel the enthusiasm and excitement. Take the message of the nuggets and challenge the words to make yourself better. Develop the habits necessary to become a great coach, the habits necessary to handle the pressure situations.

A lot of coaches have the same opportunity. Very few coaches will accept the challenge to change their habits of learning. Accept the challenge to change your habits in order to learn and improve, to look for solutions in all the situations of life, and to become a great coach. Just as you ask your players to focus, to concentrate, to accept challenge—you must first accept these things yourself.

Today, accept the pressure and the challenge of coaching.

Today your whistle has a new sound. You have discovered new solutions. The coaches who once knew you will not recognize you. Today you are a new person. Today you are a new coach. Today you accept the challenge. Today you begin anew. Your whistle sounds golden.

Develop your own process.

Develop your own style.

Change how you learn the game.

Embrace the pressure.

Change your habits.

When the pressure mounts and your habits are challenged you will say, "I will change with the times but cling to unchanging principles."

You become your habits in pressure situations.

To the Reader

Congratulations on reading the second nugget. Think about it. Let it become a part of you. Add your own thoughts. Start to develop your own process. The journey never ends.

1.   What one theme dominates this nugget?

2.   What is the mantra of this nugget?

3.   What Big Word tips off the nugget?

4.   Write down five takeaways from this nugget. Re-read as necessary.

5.   What did Ralph Waldo Emerson think about habits?

6.   If you could talk to one coach today, who would that be? What would you want to discuss?

GOLDEN NUGGET NO. 3

The Dawn Alleviates

Appreciation

Players will give you more if they know you care and if
they know you appreciate their effort.

Welcome to the third nugget. It's about appreciating
and loving yourself and the game.

'The dawn alleviates' simply means that tomorrow will be
better. Coaching can be very difficult, particularly after tough
losses or confrontations with players, other coaches, officials
or parents. Just knowing that it will get better and that the
sun will indeed come up tomorrow can help you through
those difficult moments which, if not handled properly, can
damage your coaching career.

You must develop resiliency in the face of adversity. This
is one of the greatest secrets to success in all of life and particularly in coaching. Coaches by and large represent the
macho in life. They are tough, hard-nosed and seemingly
uncaring. The image is often deserved when you look at the
old coaches–coaches who screamed and intimidated and
demanded perfection. A little toughness is understood by
everyone, but it must be preceded and followed by caring,
kindness and appreciation. If you love the game, you must
let the players know, and let them know that you'll love them
as much during the tough losses as you do in the great wins.
They must know that you have their backs.

"Weeping may last for the night, but a shout of joy
comes in the morning."
–Psalm 36:5

The dawn alleviates.

No matter how bad the day is today, no matter how bad the loss was last night, it will be better tomorrow and, with awareness, understanding and appreciation even for the bad things, which are opportunities for growth, you will continue to get better.

If all else is equal, the bigger, stronger player wins, the aggressive, hard-nosed player is an asset, the in-your-face defender makes life tough for the opponents. Yes, you need to teach this, but only true caring for each player and for the game can motivate and bring your team together so they can reach their full potential and you can really appreciate each other.

Love the game.
Love the players.
Love to be in the gym.
Love to coach.
Love to teach.

Others may question your style of play. They may wonder about your coaching strategies. Your late game decision-making may drive them to an early grave. They may reject your appearance and demeanor. Even your way of substituting during games may cause them to suspect you. Yet your consistent kindness, appreciation and caring will withstand all opposition, and eventually your opponents will become your supporters.

From the Locker Room—Little K

"Times have changed. The coach cannot
be a bully. With television, cell phones

and iPods, you must be very careful what
you say and do. Most importantly, always
do the right thing even if nobody is watching."

—Mike Tartara, Cuyahoga Heights,
Ohio high school coach and teacher

Each day you must ask, "What can I do for you?" Don't wait for the dawn to do this. Begin today. Show your appreciation to players, parents, officials, fans, administrators and opponents in all your behavior, not just your words, and they will warm to you.

The dawn alleviates.

Love the challenge of the game, because it drives you toward excellence.

Become expert in offense, for it shows great excitement.

Focus on defense, because it shows you consistency and toughness.

Accept winning humbly, for it enriches your heart.

Welcome losses, for they redirect and focus you; they open your soul.

Acknowledge honors, because they represent the team.

Ask, "What can I do to help you?"

Starting today, how will you coach?

Respect and appreciate your opponents and they will become your friends.

Work with your assistants in such a way that they will become like family.

Look for reasons to say, "Well done."

Applaud, correct, and try very hard not to complain.

Shout praise and whisper criticism.

Be tough, but be fair.

You'll still get angry. You may even lash out once in awhile. But know this: constant criticism constricts.

From the Locker Room—Little K

"One kind word from the coach can motivate a player through an entire practice."

—Alan Stein, Stronger Team

Just as you praise the heralded recruit or your best player, speak the same message to all the players, even the bench warmers. It's ok to work their butts off and discipline them when it's appropriate, but they must know that you are trying to make them better.

Polishing the Nugget

Rick was one of my all-time great players. He came from a family that had high expectations in all areas of life. His dad had coached him as a kid and made sure that he did lots of drills and other workouts at home. Rick had a lot of natural talent, averaging nineteen points per game as an ninth grade player. That summer he went to camp with lots of confidence and probably a fair amount of bragging.

He got his butt beat and sulked during the entire car ride home.

That night Rick's dad heard a thumping sound from the back deck. He looked out the window and saw Rick dribbling and shooting under the light. He asked his son what he was doing and Rick responded, "I've always done the daily dozen drills because you told me to, but from now on I'm doing them for me."

The following year he averaged forty points a game as a sophomore and led the nation in scoring.

Tomorrow will be better if you decide today to work your butt off.

Parents can be a problem. Be kind even to them even if they attack you. You will accomplish this by understanding that they love their sons or daughters more than they love you. They may be angry at you, but they also have wonderful qualities that you must discover through understanding. You need to understand that they may mistrust you. But over time and with persistent appreciation you will find ways to understand each other.

This is a real test of your class and character. You must develop habits that will help you react in the best way possible no matter how tense the situation. Being aware of problems can make you proactive and reduce negative reactions.

If they don't support you today, *the dawn alleviates* and they will support you tomorrow.

Not every player will start or get equal playing time or want to run the offense you want to run, but if you care deeply about all the players becoming better, becoming all they can in life and in the game, your attitude of caring will prevail.

From the Classroom—Coach Aupp

"A coach who really sees into the hearts
of his players knows what to overlook."

—Fred Taylor, Ohio State University coach

In order to truly appreciate, you must listen.

Listen to the players with great work ethics; they inspire you to work harder. Listen to the bench players; they teach you patience. It is easy to appreciate All-Americans who help you win, but they too need to be listened to. Listen to the average players, for there are so many of them. Listen to the seniors for experience and wisdom and to the freshmen for their wild-eyed excitement, although this makes it sometimes difficult to hear them. Move closer and listen to all the players for the joy they bring.

Listen! Change happens when you make yourself ready for it!

The criticism of fans, the confrontations with officials, the moments of hate and anger can be deflected with kindness. When things don't go your way and you encounter disappointment, your resilience will only get stronger.

Hate and anger are distractions. It's ok to be negative at times or to challenge people and players with tough love. But be careful how and when you do this and be extremely aware why you are doing it.

The repetitive practices, the challenging games, the long tiring season with its ups and downs will be made easier when you focus on listening and appreciating. Doing this today will make tomorrow easier.

The dawn alleviates.

Walk with your head up when you win and when you lose. Confront everyone the same way: with kindness and with understanding. If they confront you with anger and disappointment, take a deep breath and say, "Thank you. What can I do to make it better?"

When you meet someone who is angry or upset, first think to yourself, "Thank you. I appreciate you even in your anger." Then say to them, "How can I help you?" This will melt the anger in their hearts and allow you to look at each other as equals. This will not be easy, but it is a challenge worth accepting.

To learn this new habit of appreciation of others, begin with yourself. Emphasize kindness and understanding:

1. I will respect my body. I will not overeat. I will not snack out of anger or frustration. I will stay away from fast food. I will be more selective about my salt, fat and sugar intake.

2. I will be an eternal listener and learner, seeking knowledge from all people and places I travel.

3. I will carefully choose the words I speak and the companions I seek. The Big Word Offense shows itself again.

4. I will be patient with myself when I fall short of my own expectations, but I will not give up. I will keep on trying and doing the best I can.

5. When I feel discouraged, I will remember that tomorrow's dawn will alleviate.

Commit yourself to the game and the players. Share your commitment through listening, kindness and appreciation to everyone around you in all circumstances. Appreciate all your blessings each day. And always ask, "How can I help me–help you?"

The dawn alleviates.

To the Reader

Congratulations on completing the third nugget.

1. What is the main theme of nugget three?

2. What mantra will you carry with you?

3. What Big Word will you start with?

4. Love of the game, having a passion to learn and knowing yourself will help you become a better coach. If you trust the players and they trust you, this will help your team become better. Write down how loving can make you a better coach.

5. Don't you just love the tremendous challenge of coaching? Do you appreciate the game?

6. Before you turn to Nugget #4, add a quote to be passed on to other coaches.

GOLDEN NUGGET NO. 4

Desire Deters Failure

Perseverance

The secret of perseverance is to apply your physical, mental and emotional talents to solving problems, day after day, without losing your desire.

The fourth nugget is about your desire to coach. Do you really have a passion for the game of basketball? Can you handle the losses and the long, tough nights of doubt? All coaches go through tough times. If you have prepared well, you will not surrender easily. Know the game and know yourself. Know your players. Know that you must be tough.

It's not the actual coaching you do (the X and O's) that is really important. It's the energy, the vision, the determination and the mindset that you bring to your team every day that really matters. You must really want to coach.

To accept the challenge of seeking knowledge, you must have a passion for the game. Passion, desire and determination are difficult to teach and to learn. They are often acquired in the school of hard knocks. Do not be deterred. Your desire, your purpose and your passion must be bigger than the obstacles and challenges that you will face. Conquer your doubts and build your desire with love and preparation.

Prepare, practice and persevere.

Polishing the Nugget

I remember Gordon telling me about his oral exam in law school. They asked, "What course did you take in college that helped you best prepare to become a lawyer?"

Without hesitation, he answered, "Basketball. I learned to work hard in spite of not getting to play much. I learned to help the starting players get better. I learned that, no matter what your role in the team might be, you must think it is the most important role on the team."

How many of you coaches have players on your team like Gordon? The great kid; smart but not a great player. Those are the ones with great desire that can spread to every player on the team. You need the great players, the starters, but you must also coach and teach and keep the players whose desire is contagious and who can make a difference in the long run.

Today, Gordon laughs when we talk about being "All Big Ten" because he scored a total of ten points his senior year. But he led the league in desire and perseverance—he helped the team become all it could be.

Are you preparing the Gordons on your team?

Desire deters failure.

The game creates stress, it creates tension, it creates adversarial roles and a heated competitive environment. Without a strong heart or a great will to keep working and keep getting better, the faint of heart will falter. In the middle of crisis you must simple-size your choices and your decision-making.

What do I mean by 'simple-size?' Don't complicate things. Put things in proper order; find a sequence. Don't take on too many projects at one time. To be successful at simple-sizing, be sure to keep your focus and keep your eyes on your goals. You must do what is necessary to make yourself better.

From the classroom—Coach Aupp

> "Our doubts are our traitors. They
> make us lose the good we oft'
> might win by fearing to attempt."
>
> > —William Shakespeare "Measure for Measure,"
> > Act 1, Scene 4

Solution-based basketball is built on recognizing and understanding problems, asking the right questions, always seeking the best answers, and being able to persevere. Basketball can build attitude and character and it can just as easily tear it down. It's not the basketball, it's the people.

Welcome the challenge.

Some people will call it heart, some mental toughness, some persistence, but no matter what you call it, it cannot be given to you. You must earn it. You must have the desire to be happy in the game and then create that joy of the game in your players.

From the Office—Coach Faylor

> "Not all coaches and players start out with the
> passion to be great, but all coaches and players
> need to develop it. The coach must have a great
> desire to know the game and be able to pass this
> knowledge on to the players. The coach must be
> able to motivate players to new levels! The coach
> must have passion to do this."
>
> > —Glenn Wilkes, Stetson University (Florida) coach
> > and professor

Desire deters failure and motivates the coach and his players.

Be bold and be wise.

It is better if each player would light his own fire, but you know this does not always happen. So you must be prepared to light the fire for them so they can burn with desire for the game. Be a coach in pursuit of the golden whistle and develop the solutions to do that.

You need great desire to light the fire of desire in your players!

You can enhance your desire with the necessary tools and knowledge of the game. Share those tools and your knowledge with your players in order to enhance their desire. You must believe in yourself and believe in the players.

You must possess desire and passion to learn the game and pass it on to the players.

Desire is more than enthusiasm or positivism. A player may guard with such enthusiasm that he fouls out constantly. A coach may run practice with encouraging words but no discipline or structure. Desire that can sustain you throughout a demanding coaching career is founded on knowledge, skills and experience. This is the kind of desire that you will always be able to draw strength from even in the worst of times, desire that will always fuel your perseverance, desire that will permeate your teams year after year.

Desire can be caught and taught by example. Desire allows players to practice hard to maintain focus and to build their fundamentals. Be the best teacher you can be so that you can motivate the players to reach new heights.

You will be tested daily in practice. The challenge is great indeed. Can you accept turnovers and yet strive to get better and learn from each situation? You must show tough love and fan the embers of each player's desire into a bright burning flame of passion that takes on a life of its own.

Simple-size your choices, your decision-making and your life. Can you do this?

You must be able to get into the players' heads and their hearts. By doing this, you will be able to teach values of caring, giving, sharing, goodness, truth, loyalty, honesty. These words are all part of the Big Word Offense. Your desire and your passion determine your path. Know yourself. Know that your words are powerful.

Desire deters failure.

From the Classroom—Coach Aupp

> "The mark of a good teacher/coach is the ability
> to simplify subject matter and motivate his players."
>
> –Ralph Miller, Oregon State coach

Prepare, practice, simple-size your life and persevere with passion.

From the Locker Room—Little K

> "You will be tested every day.
> How you respond will depend on your
> preparation and understanding of all
> the situations and circumstances involved
> in the game of basketball."
>
> —Ken Padfield, Muskingum University (Ohio)
> coach and teacher

Be like the player who jumps rope every day and little by little his vertical jump increases. Or the player who benches 120 pounds twenty times and finally gets to twenty-one and gains added strength. Or the player who shoots extra every night and becomes an eighty percent-plus foul shooter. Be the coach who makes ten recruiting calls and after practice makes two more and gets his best recruit.

You need to help the players understand one on one, two on two, three on three, four on four, and all the fundamentals until, through endless repetition, these many attempts come together, one fundamental at a time, eventually uniting all five individuals into a true team. You must teach individual fundamentals and team strategies.

Be strong so you can lift the players out of their moments of frustration.

Endure all complications, problems and crises.

Challenge the obstacles that surround you.

Know that where preparation and perspiration meet you encounter inspiration.

Prepare until you succeed in out-working every opponent.

Keep your eyes on your goals.

There are no failures. There are only those who have quit trying.

Desire deters failure.

You must have the desire to teach more than just the game of basketball. Your desire must also embrace teaching beyond the X's and O's:

1. Communication skills, particularly listening

2. Relationship-building

3. How to work and sacrifice

4. How to act and how to interact

5. How to react; self-control

6. How to deal with adversity of all kinds

7. How to deal with social pressure, including drugs, alcohol and sex

8. How to react to change

9. How to have faith

Continue to engage the nuggets and apply their secrets. Act on your desire to learn from the great coaches about this great game. Do not be deterred.

One of the secrets is that it is not about knowledge alone; but knowledge coupled with perseverance can win the day. Make one more phone call; talk to one more recruit. Stay and help a player with his shooting. By staying the extra moment, you gain an advantage over those who leave at a determined time. Be smart and save time for your family.

The ability to bounce back, to turn bad breaks into opportunities, is a trait nearly all successful coaches possess. They simply will not be defeated. You must live and work with great enthusiasm. When the challenges and obstacles start to enhance failure and you are getting overwhelmed, just remember there are always lessons to be learned and opportunities to grow and become better. Remember—there are a lot of Gordons on your team.

From the Locker Room—Little K

> "The good teams never cross the finish line."

> —George Raveling, Nike Director of
> International Basketball, coach and teacher

Desire deters failure.

From the Office—Coach Faylor

> "If you have talent, you will receive a
> good measure of success, but only if you
> persist."

> —Isaac Asimov, author

Your desire, united with your team's desire, will deter failure.

How can you sustain your desire as a coach so you can 'bring it' year after year to your players? Keep learning, keep growing, keep coming back to these nuggets to help you feel your desire.

To the Reader

1. What is the theme of nugget 4?

2. What is the mantra?

3. What Big Word leads the fast break?

4. How can perseverance help you become the best coach you can be?

5. What is Solution-Based Basketball?

6. Your desire will show in the tough moments. Do an inventory of your desire to be a great coach. Are you really preparing yourself?

7. Can you become a Golden Whistle coach? I'll answer that for you: Yes! Now, tell me how.

GOLDEN NUGGET NO. 5
Put the Beating Stick Down

Patience

When the players just don't seem to get it; when you are on a losing
streak; when you go home and your children act up; when the
president or principal calls you into his office; you must have
patience. Watching another coach win and not playing the
blame game and not disliking (or even hating) him for
his glory requires you to have patience and class.

This nugget has special value for coaches who wear their
emotions on their sleeves. If you're honest with yourself, you'll know this includes you. It's certainly true for me,
because as a young coach, when I lost I took it out on any-
body and everybody. The officials I berated, the parents I got
mad at, my family who was always waiting for me to show up
and often I didn't, all certainly deserved to be handled with
more class.

I certainly could have used the advice I'm giving a lot
sooner in my career. I hope you will learn this lesson quicker
than I did.

The intensity and competitive nature of the game will
bring out the true qualities not only of the coach and of the
players but also the fans and the parents. The problem is that
these can be both good and bad. You must learn to handle
them. It's not about you vs. them. It's just the way the game
is. You must develop patience.

As coaches, we are sometimes extremely hard on ourselves and on our players. At times, we place too much emphasis on winning and losing for fear of losing our jobs. Every day we need to accept the challenge to become a better teacher/coach and to help every player improve so that they can reach their full potential.

You must put the beating stick down.

We can panic too easily, particularly after a tough loss. Out comes the beating stick. Beating ourselves up is bad enough, but then we start to swing the stick around and hurt those around us. The players can feel the sting. Our spouses, our families, even the officials know when our beating stick is out. The only known antidote and prevention is to say, "Put the beating stick down, not just for myself, but for everyone concerned."

From the Classroom—Coach Aupp

> Because coaching basketball is so dynamic
> and challenging, it will reveal the true character
> of the coach and the player.
>
> –John Bunn, Stanford University coach

Always remember that problems and concerns are a continuous part of every coach's life. Don't take yourself so seriously that it inflicts pain on others.

Polishing the Nugget

I remember a mom confronting me after a game in a way only a mom, who loves her son more than she loves me, can. She was vehement in her attack on my character, saying things we all like to hear like, "You're ruining my son." "He should be playing more." "He never gets a chance." "You're terrible." She had her beating stick out and didn't care if she beat me to death with it.

Being young and foolish and lacking any **patience** after a tough loss, I grabbed my own beating stick, which was bigger than hers, and told her what I thought about her and her son. I then proceeded to her son and told him what she had done and told him to meet me in my office at eight the next morning.

We talked. Rather, I talked, and we both decided it would be best for him not to play any longer. I decided and reacted with anger and ego and pride. Eventually I learned from that and grew from that, but I cost a young man a chance to play. He may not have ever played a lot, but I beat him with my stick and he had no chance.

Put your beating stick down.

It is easy to lose perspective as to what is really important. Those around you can tell when the beating stick is out, even though the stick is invisible. It's embarrassing to remember the times when we've jumped up and down or have run along the sidelines screaming, ranting, raving and even swearing at officials. You know your beating stick has been out when you've torn off your coat and gotten into the faces of the players, accosting them for their bad play. Or the awful time when you were on your hands and knees pounding the floor after a tough loss. I remember the time I carried the stick to the post-game press conference and said things that I've regretted ever since. We have all been there and beaten ourselves up.

I will put the beating stick down. Will you?

If you can grin in the face of adversity your attitude will improve. You must know that you're not alone. The national average for wins and losses each game night is fifty percent. Can you see a bigger picture and not just feel sorry for yourself?

Learn to laugh at yourself and with those around you, because everyone will benefit. The players will start to grin and work even harder. Your family will accept the tough times by sharing your laughter, and all those who know you will become more accepting of who you are.

From the Classroom—Coach Aupp

> "Laugh and the world laughs with you.
> Lose with a smile and you will not lose alone."
>
> —Irene Horner, Muskingum University (Ohio) coach and teacher

It is difficult to maintain patience and have a good attitude when even those closest to you seem to turn against you—when players make excuses, when parents question your coaching, when your family thinks you spend too much time away. They will test the patience of any coach.

You need to learn to say eight words that will help you find patience and to respond in a caring, positive manner. Practice these words so that in each negative situation they will be an automatic reaction. Remember them. This will keep you from bringing out your beating stick.

Say these eight words over and over when you reach for your beating stick. This has been a mantra of mine for years. Even the toughest losses can help you if you continue to work hard.

> *The wind in the world blows toward good,*
> *(if you don't pick up your beating stick too quickly.)*

This is a lot like the old 'count to ten before speaking' method. It will help you gain patience so you don't fly off the handle too quickly.

Where is the team who won the first NCAA championship? Where is the building they played in at Northwestern University? The records of today's greatest coaches will be exceeded by the next generation. If all things pass, why should we be too concerned about today? Because it's important today to work hard, persist, and to prepare, so that when things go wrong you can say,

> *The wind in the world blows toward good.*
> *I'll put the beating stick down*
> *and pick up a smile.*

Walk on the court every day with a smile and wrap each practice in joy. Know the now. If you can do that, you will never work hard to be happy; instead you'll be too busy in practice to be sad. Cherish today's victories today, enjoy their moment and let them go. We can talk a good game. We can talk about passion and purpose. But it speaks volumes when we live them.

You can't store wins in your travel bag; enjoy them and let them go. You cannot save time outs for another game; use them as needed and then let them go and do not think about them again. The game, win or lose, must be played today. Try to enjoy it, challenge it, prepare for it, love it, hate it, whatever your emotion shows, then let it go. Little by little you will become more patient.

Polishing the Nugget

Several years later, in a very similar situation to the preceding story, after a difficult loss, a mother confronted me about her son's playing time, when would he start playing more, and how bad a coach I was. Her anger at me was tethered to her love for her son.

I looked at her, leaned down and kissed her on her forehead and said, "I love your son and he will get to play more when he is ready." With tears in her eyes, she said, "I'm sorry" and gave me a hug.

Her son didn't play much that year, but became an All-Conference player the following year. **Patience** prevents the beating stick from even being picked up.

The wind in the world blows toward good. Always.

With this knowledge and with your smile all things will be reduced to their proper perspective.

Be joyful about your victories but stay humble. You will hurt when you lose, but remember that the wind in the world blows toward good. When people criticize what you are doing, change the way they feel with your smile. Do not take things too personally. It is not You versus Them. Your patience will allow you to look behind the moment and not make rash or foolish decisions.

Each day will bring true joy only when your smile brings forth smiles from all those around you. Even those who do not believe in you will be won over by that great smile.

In the middle of chaos and confusion, you can maintain a calm heart if you can smile and embrace the moment. You will enhance your teaching and coaching. Patience delays reactions.

Just as a great pass sets up the shooter ... or a great penetration and pass can lead to a lay up ... or a great hustle on defense can sustain you on a bad shooting night ... laughter will lighten the load in coaching. Your increased patience will be calming to your players, particularly in a tough, tight game.

From the Classroom—Coach Aupp

"A smile creates confidence.
A smile with a kind word creates friendship.
A smile with a kind word and a helping
hand creates love."
—Lao-Tzu

When you have learned to be patient and even to laugh at yourself, at bad calls, at turnovers, at criticism, at the trials and tests of coaching, nothing can defeat you.

With patience, you will be happy. You will be successful.

Put the beating stick down and pick up a smile. Become the greatest coach you can possibly be.

To the Reader

1. What is the theme of nugget 5?

2. What is the mantra?

3. What is the Big Word?

4. Did you get the purpose of this chapter? Could you see yourself over-reacting?

5. Write down a couple of times that you can remember whipping out the beating stick.

6. "In coaching you must face the opponent inside you. He is far more dangerous and will defeat you more quickly than anyone else can." Explain this statement and give one example of how this might work.

GOLDEN NUGGET NO. 6

Choose to Get Better Every Day

Choices

What time do you get up every day?
Do you start the day working on the game of basketball?
Are you doing what you want or what others want you to do?
How can you increase your value and earn your golden whistle?
It really seems quite simple: make good choices, make good decisions.

My grandmother took rags of no value and sewed them into magnificent quilts of great value. She did it with time and patience and love. Today her quilts are priceless; not perhaps in money, but most definitely in wonderful memories.

Will you increase your value? How will you be remembered? By choosing to get better every day, you are positioning for the possible!

It's our choices, not the conditions we find ourselves in, that will determine our coaching careers. No matter how hectic and busy and occupied your life gets, you need to challenge yourself each day to increase your knowledge and understanding of the game. The coach must choose to get better every day to increase his knowledge. The coach must be trained in all aspects of the game. You would not want a doctor or lawyer who was not trained and who did not want to continue to get better to operate on you or defend you in a trial.

Get better today and tomorrow do the same and every tomorrow for the rest of your life.

The choice is yours.

A young player who shoots "around the world shots" every day becomes a Jerry Lucas.

A young player who practices ball-handling and plays against older players to make himself tougher becomes Bob Cousy.

A young player who gets cut from his high school team becomes a Michael Jordan.

A young coach who loves the game and increases his knowledge each day becomes the greatest coach he can be and earns his golden whistle.

A young group of players touched by the genius of that great coach increases their talent and becomes a great team.

They all made the choice to become great. They made the choice to take actions every day that help them grow and that over time will help them become great.

If it's possible for young players to increase their game through hard work combined with talent, then it is also possible for you to become all you are capable of becoming as a coach.

Continue to grow as a coach so you can help each player grow and together you can make a great team.

Today, choose to increase your awareness and understanding. Through this, you can lift your players to increase their skills.

How can you accomplish this? By making good choices. If you want to be sure that a choice is a good one, measure it against your objectives. You must first have specific objectives before you can decide which choices are right or wrong. This is how coaching can bear the fruits of victory.

From the Locker Room—Little K

"A player must be pushed and challenged before he can grow to new levels. Players

don't always want to push themselves as
hard as you want them to. That's a great
coaching challenge: Help the players want
to make the choice to become great."

—Ganon Baker, Elev8 Sports Institute

From the Locker Room—Little K

"I will take the hardest day I have ever
worked in my life and make that my average."

—Ed Sherman, Muskingum University
football coach and professor

As a teacher and as a coach, it's important to set your goals
high and have your players set their goals high. You must be
realistic, but you must set your goals high. Isn't it better to
aim high on the bankboard in life and still have a chance that
the ball will go in? In that way, isn't it better that you strive for
an undefeated season and accept the pain of one defeat than
not try because you think your goals are too high?

Today, choose to aim high and increase your caring
for yourself and your players.

Do not let the height of your goals hold you back. Even
though you may run into walls of criticism and defeat, stand
tall each time you are challenged. If you are to earn your
golden whistle, you must learn from each loss and find a way
to increase your position and your value in coaching.

Polishing the Nugget

I was in graduate school getting an advanced degree
and chasing my dream of being a great teacher and coach.
I did this for more than ten summers, driving eighty miles

each way to the university and staying in that city Monday through Friday for my classes. I was not aware of the real impact this was having on my family. To put it simply, "I was not there enough."

One Friday, a class was canceled and I got to go home early. I arrived about 1:30 in the afternoon and nobody was home. I knew my wife took the kids to the pool, so I drove up. I spotted them right away. My wife was pulling a wagon with both children in it up a steep hill. She looked exhausted. I pulled up and cheerfully called out, "Surprise!" I got that 'I've had the kids for five straight days' look; somewhere between desperation and anger. I parked the car and went to help. She snapped, "I can do it. I do it all the time." I replied, "I'm sorry I am gone so much. I'm doing this for the family." She gave me 'that look' again and said, "You do it for your own ego. Remember this: every day that you spend getting your degree is one day less that you get to spend with me and the kids. They are growing up in front of you and you are not getting to share that with them. Go chase your damn dreams. I've had it!"

Wow! That put me back on my heels. I was really unaware of just how much I had neglected them. I had some choices that needed to be made and one of them I made right there. I needed to value, respect and spend more time with my family. This was a choice I never regretted.

It's important in your own chase to engage in the little everyday wonderment of family. That day I made the greatest coach's decision of my life: to invest in my family.

It didn't take much. I started coming home in the middle of the week to help take care of the kids. I also took my wife out to eat and arranged for the babysitter. I never felt our marriage was in doubt, but the quality of our marriage became better because of my awareness.

From the Locker Room—Little K

"Never waste your failures."

—Kevin Eastman, Los Angeles Clippers
assistant coach

Those coaches who carry defeat with them in their back pockets with worry, concern and anger will not see ways to improve. They will lose sight of their goals. A victory drought of just a couple of games can destroy them. They are setting themselves up to fail and they don't know why.

Do not be that coach. Remember that **desire deters failure**. Find a way to harvest positive thoughts in the barren desert of defeat. See your goals through to the end.

Let the other coaches cry in their defeat. You are too busy finding ways to win by learning, growing and gaining deeper understanding of yourself, your players and the game. Gain confidence by harvesting good from bad and increase your value with each practice, each lesson, each game—win or lose.

Today, choose to get better as a coach and as a teacher.

Choose to create a culture of greatness even in defeat and understand that if the team and the players are to change and get better, the coach must first choose to get better himself and to change himself.

Today, commit to the choice of getting better every day and commit yourself to challenging and motivating all your players to improve their game. Today, be smarter than yesterday. Prepare for each practice, for each game, for each season, using all your knowledge and skills. Challenge yourself today so you can be better tomorrow.

How can you decrease your value? Make poor choices like these:

1. Do not continue to learn and grow. Keep the status quo.

2. Do the same things you did last year.

3. Close your mind to new ideas.

4. Want to win more than you want to help players.

5. Become negative and reactionary

6. Be on the referees constantly.

7. Dislike parents, fans and administrators.

8. Set your expectations excessively high or set no expectations at all.

9. Worry about your own image.

10. Try to do everything yourself.

11. Neglect your family.

12. Reject technology. (added by Little K)

Increase your value as a coach, but maintain your integrity. Work hard and increase your knowledge and you will get better every day.

Work hard and smart today and when the day is done, work harder and smarter tomorrow. As your value as a coach increases, the sound of your whistle will be increasingly golden, and all who hear it will increase in value too.

Choose to get better every day.
The choice is really yours.

To the Reader

1. What is the theme of nugget 6?

2. What is the mantra?

3. What's the Big Word?

4. How good do you want to be?

5. How can you become a better coach? By choosing to get better every day.

6. How important are your choices?

7. What does positioning for the possible mean to you?

GOLDEN NUGGET NO. 7

Circumstances and Situations Be Damned

Challenge

There will always be problems that are out of your control. You must face up to them and truly accept them.

Challenge

Always find a lesson or gift and grow from any difficulties you encounter.

Challenge

Find the unique gifts that only you possess.

Challenge

Dig deeply and know your true purpose as a coach.

This nugget is so important because in life and in coaching we tend to blame everything on circumstances and situations. Anything at all besides ourselves. The players don't care, the fans are terrible, the parents only care about their own son or daughter, the officials are horrible. I think you get the idea. Things will happen and you have no control. But you <u>can</u> control and change how you think and react. You can change, you can adjust. You can become a better coach.

We can't stop the wind in the world from blowing bad times into our lives. We can't stop losses from occurring or bad calls from officials or fans or parents from getting on us, but we can control our emotions and reactions. This is a great challenge. But you can believe that 'The wind in the world always blows toward good.' Your purpose as a coach is letting your character run further than any circumstance or situation you encounter.

Circumstances and situations be damned.
I will learn how to control my thoughts and reactions.
What a great challenge.

SNAP YOUR FINGERS

"Snap your fingers." I told my players every year before the season to snap their fingers and that's how fast their careers go. The practice starts, the practice ends. The season starts, the season ends. Players are freshmen and then they are seniors. Some stay the same, some become unbelievable. The fans cheer, the fans boo. The wins come, the losses sneak in. The referee makes a call and it's good or bad, depending on which side you are on. We are in preseason—how did the postseason workout get here? The shot goes up—sometimes it goes in. The defense advances, the defense retreats. A player starts, a sub comes in. The game is played and the coaches coach. You are young and then you are old. One thing is for sure, it flies by. Snap your fingers and it's over. Some things you can control; some you cannot.

But you can always work harder to control your emotions.

All games and seasons flow in a circle of attitudes and reactions to situations and circumstances. As a coach, you are a part of the game, so like the seasons your attitude will rise in the moment of a great steal and fall with a missed layup. If you want your players' emotions and reactions to be good, look in the mirror.

Polishing the Nugget

I saw something in Chester that even he didn't see. My assistant coach wanted to get rid of him. "He's too small, too weak, he can't shoot it a lick. Why would you want to keep him?" I responded, "He has a great heart and he works hard. I see him in two years being a good player."

Chester played JV for two years behind a very good point guard. He worked hard, never complained and got bigger and stronger. He worked on his shot, but his real strength was in handling the ball and getting it to our best players. He led by example, he lifted everyone, including me, and became an All-League player his last two seasons.

You must look at yourself as a coach. Can you see the potential in a player? Don't just look at his size or strength or jumping, but check the size of his heart.

Chester made me believe in his great heart.

Today, learn how to change and adjust.

FICKLE FANS

Every day that you coach, you go to practice with thoughts that have changed from yesterday. Yesterday's joy from winning will become today's frustration of a practice when the players are complacent. But today's complacency can fade into tomorrow's greatness when you learn to recognize and combat these challenges.

Inside all of us is a hoop that constantly revolves from disappointment to joy, sometimes with each missed shot or poor defensive rotation. Our mood goes up and down like a yo-yo and goes in circles like a hula hoop—from happiness to sadness in a heartbeat, especially during games.

You must be aware that this is the nature of the game; it has ups and downs and you need to be ready to handle the swift and constant changes.

The fickle fans' expressions of joy to you after today's great win will flip into harsh words with the next loss. Remember that, like you, each fan has a rotating hoop of varying emotions inside. Accept the fans for who they are and be in control of your emotions no matter how they react.

Be tough. Be loving. Challenge the players. Work hard. Be consistent. You must constantly learn new ways to control your temper. Do not surrender your passion or your feelings, but transcend* your attitude to meet the needs of the team, the players and all those involved.

Today let circumstances and situations be damned. I will learn to control my temper.

HOW DO YOU REACT?

Are you prepared to face the following emotionally charged situations?

1. A parent of one of the players gets in your face after the game, calls you names, and in front of the team tells you how bad a coach you are. How will you react? Are you ready for this? This situation can happen whether you win or lose.

2. The late charge call that shows in the film replay that the player definitely moved. How do you keep from screaming and swearing and chasing after the official as he leaves the floor? Oh, this moment will come for sure. Will you have the poise and discipline you want your players to have? Will you react in a positive way? It's ok to react negatively, but there must be control.

---

*   Did you look up 'transcend?'

3. You answer the phone and the voice says, "I've decided not to come to your school. I'm going to be playing against you next year." The emotions will surface. The desire to react and curse or demean the player and the other team will arise. How will you respond? Are you ready for the moment?

Remember that you're not alone. Coaches go through this every day, every week, every year. Remember that it's not about what happens, but how you react.

Polishing the Nugget

Why are some memories so clear? The entire game is still vivid in my mind. It was a road game, a long trip in cold, snowy weather.

In those days there were just two officials for the games. One of the officials that evening was nearly sixty. Very old! But he had a great reputation; he had even officiated at the 1948 Olympic Games.

I was not impressed. It seemed he just couldn't keep up with the plays. Early in the game, someone in the crowd threw a fish on the floor (our team mascot was the Muskie), which delayed the game. I asked him about a technical and he just smiled. Later in the very competitive game, a group of students came in and had a sit-in to protest something, which again delayed the game. I mentioned to the official in a stern voice, "You don't think that might deserve a technical?" He answered, "You coach; I'll officiate." Of course, for the rest of the game I didn't coach much, but spent the time yelling at him.

We won a close game and I still chased him into the official's locker room yelling things like, "You're too old to officiate. You need to get out of the game" and that he was terrible. He let me vent and then said mildly, "Good win. You are lucky, because you spent way too much time worrying about me and things you can't control and not coaching." He continued in a very calm voice, "You are a good young coach, but if you want me to officiate better, coach your team better. They were out of control because you were out of control. Let's see if both of us can't continue to try and be better."

Of course he was right. I let the situation and circumstances of the game control my emotions. He taught me a valuable lesson: control what you can and adjust to what you can't.

Circumstances and situations be damned.
Find the gifts hidden in your fears.

NEGATIVE VS. POSITIVE

The challenge is great indeed. How can you master these negative emotions? If all you do is hold them in, they erupt in an even bigger explosion. You must realize that your negative reactions are all fears. You must learn to accept this. When you feel your blood boil or your stomach churn, ask yourself, "What am I afraid of right now?"

Unless your attitude is positive, the day, the practice, the game, the season will be a failure. The game can change so quickly, and often you have no control. But you have the power to make your own decisions and choose your own attitudes and you can carry them with you wherever you go.

If you have a negative or pessimistic attitude in practice, particularly after a loss, the players will react with doubt and despair. The amazing thing is you can carry this to your family in the same way and wonder why you get the cold shoulder from your spouse.

If you exude joy, enthusiasm, excitement and a positive spirit of excitement in spite of any circumstances and situations, you will receive that back a hundredfold from your players and your family. Your attitude and emotions will produce positive emotions from all you come into contact with.

In all this, you must be authentic. You might fool others, but you cannot fool yourself. "Mirror, mirror on the wall; I am that person after all."

I will understand and accept my fears
and control my emotions
and this will bear buckets of golden nuggets of love.

Refuse to let circumstances and situations in life control the way you respond and how you treat people.

From the Classroom—Coach Aupp

> "It matters not how strait the gate,
> How charged with punishments the scroll
> I am the master of my fate:
> I am the captain of my soul."
>
> —from "Invictus" by William Ernest Henley

ARE YOU IN CONTROL OR JUST DEPRESSED?

Are you in control? How will you control your emotions so that even after losses, after disappointments, every day is a joyous day, a productive day, a day in which you don't swing the beating stick and knock the love out of everyone you see? Can you control your language? This is difficult for many coaches. You must discipline yourself if you expect the players to have discipline. Instead of saying, "That's just the way it is," you must say, "What's the way it could become? I have the power to change the way it is."

Do you accept the challenge? Are you the captain of your soul?

Of course you will have problems and negative reactions. It is in the nature of the game and it's in the nature of being human. The swing of emotions from beginning to end makes it difficult to react in a positive way in every situation. But you should constantly strive to see the value of damage control and proactive thinking.

You will get depressed, you will be sad, you will yell some things you wish you could catch and pull back, you will doubt yourself, you will feel fear, you will suffer and not want to see or speak to anyone. You will put yourself in isolation and feel sorry and lost.

When that happens, take a deep breath, take a step back and take a moment to regroup. Force a smile, which might even allow you to laugh at yourself. Step back out of the moment and forgive the players, the other coach, the fans, the officials and any parent who is upset. Greet them with kindness. Approach them and put them at ease. Do not, at least for long, throw yourself a pity party. Rise above the situation and lift all of those around you.

This may be one of the biggest challenges to becoming a great coach: lift others in tough and difficult situations. In order to do that, you must first control and lift yourself. Make this one of your goals.

From the Locker Room—Little K

> "Attitude influences your emotion
> Emotions influence feelings
> Feelings influence action
> Actions influence results."
>
> —Bill Brown, Wittenberg University (Ohio) coach

THE BOOMERANG

When you begin to make these changes, you'll find that even after losses and frustrations you know that you can always be better. Do not let such things as despair, sadness or mean-spirited people affect your attitude. But there will be days when you must constantly struggle against situations and circumstances which would tear you down. When that happens, redouble your efforts to help another person, face your fears and find ways to change the circumstances and situations into golden nuggets. Like a boomerang, when you throw out love and kindness to others, it always comes back to you.

Circumstances and situations be damned.
Today, learn to communicate with love.

You will lose a game. This will allow you to prepare for the next one.

You will become angry at a player. This will allow you to work on your patience.

When the season starts to wear on you, you can find someone who cares.

When nothing seems worth it, you will find value and gratitude and joy waiting at home, if you bring it home with you.

When you are at the end of your rope, go lasso someone to love.

When you can't change a call, you can change your reaction to it.

Know your heart. Know that you matter.

You will know that you are on the path to success by the way you control your emotions. There will always be moments when you must constantly fight to control your emotions against the forces that challenge you each day as a coach. You must be aware that the challenge is there for every coach. You are not alone.

From the Office—Coach Faylor

> "I can't change what life brings or how
> people respond to my teaching and
> coaching, but I can always react with class."
>
> —Delbert Oberteuffer, author and
> Ohio State University professor

CONFIDENT OR COCKY?

Even as you win, other reactions, like cockiness and ego, can cause problems. When you do win, people will praise you and lavish you with compliments, people will want to be your friend and journalists will want to interview you. Even these can be harmful. They can make you feel that you alone are the reason for the team being successful. Be aware of the Big Head syndrome.

When overconfident from victory, remember your losses.

When your head swells, remember how little you really know.

When you focus on moments of greatness, remind yourself of moments you got your butt kicked.

When you feel all-powerful, try to change an official's call.

When you achieve greatness, always remember and be guided by your humble beginnings.

With this growing knowledge and growing self-awareness, you will also have a deeper understanding of the players you coach who have within them the same rotating hoop of emotions that you do. They will make mistakes, they will be frustrated, at times they will be irritated and irritating. Don't react negatively to the problems they bring with them to practice because that will only make it worse. Use your new skills to make a challenging situation better. Build emotional awareness in your players and handle each situation and circumstance with a positive and lifting attitude.

Develop patience and don't condemn a player on one practice or one reaction or one bad play. Try to help a player today and tomorrow even if he greets you with apprehension and dislike today. In today's practice he may not buy into the role you want him to take. Yet if you both want the same thing, he can help the team. Be patient and help with his understanding.

Sometimes as a coach you need to be thrown out of your comfort zone. This is often at the exact time that you will need to help a player back into his.

Today your players, your family, your friends and all you meet will know that you have learned to control your reactions better. Your whistle is turning into gold.

It is not the situations and circumstances in which we are placed that determines our wins or losses. Rather it is the spirit in which we handle them.

> *Circumstances and situations be damned!*
> *Circumstances and situations be blessed.*
> *I get to officiate my own game.*
> *I get to make the call.*
> *I am the captain of my soul.*

To the Reader

1. What is the theme of nugget 7?

2. What is the mantra?

3. What's the Big Word?

4. It's easy to make the call when the pressure is off. Look at your coaching career. How have you handled the pressure situations and the bad circumstances?

5. Is it ok to react negatively? How can you learn to stop your negative reactions?

6. Is it ok to say, "That's just the way I am?" How might you learn to focus on self-improvement?

7. Can you prepare ahead for all the situations and circumstances you will face in coaching? If not, can you at least prepare better?

8. Can you explain the meaning of the quote from "Invictus" by William Ernest Henby?

9. What is the Big Word Boomerang?

GOLDEN NUGGET NO. 8

Do It—Do It Right—Do It Right Now

Focus

Concentrate on what needs to be done and when it needs to be done.
Bring into vision, concentrate, converge your thoughts into one
specific area.

A lot of people talk a good game. A lot of coaches can tell you how much they know and how good a coach they are. But the truth is in the action. Your ability to learn the game is nothing without a plan of action and your ability to focus.

Do it!

You must get started. What will you focus on? In basketball you can focus on offense or defense or basic fundamentals. You must start somewhere and build on that every day.

Do it right.

You need to know what you will teach. Know what is right. Seek help. Do you teach the 1-2 stop or the 2-foot stop? Both will work. You must decide and teach what you believe. Sometimes the rules are wrong, so do it right. How? Look to your heart to know what's right.

Do it right now.

You can't wait until next year, until next season, until next week or until tomorrow. You must focus all your attention on getting started today. Right now. Don't let yourself procrastinate.

It's so easy to feel sorry for yourself—the long hours, the long season, the ups and downs of the coach's life, but you must focus on the good, the positive, the things that make coaching basketball the greatest profession in the world.

No game plan, however meticulously prepared, has ever carried a coach to victory over even one opponent. No scouting report, no matter how extensive and deep in detail, has prevented one loss. Never has there been a nugget such as the one you now read which has earned so much as an extra basket or produced a single point on the scoreboard. Words are good and powerful, but even the Big Word Offense words must be followed by action and doing. Gather your information, determine your needs and focus your attention on what must be done first. Do it.

> *It matters not how much I know unless I turn*
> *my knowledge into doing.*

Every coach has dreams and aspirations, but they will be unrealized if you don't do it now and you don't do it right. The goal to become the greatest coach is impossible unless you focus on what needs to be done today and do it.

> *I will do it.*
> *I will do it right.*
> *I will do it right now.*

All your aspirations of becoming a great coach are lost unless they are followed by your focus on creating a game plan, preparing a scouting report or studying this nugget. Purposeful preparation has already been mentioned. It is a key to getting better.

I will do it.
I will do it right.
I will do it right now.

Learn from the past, be excited about the future, but execute today. This is the beginning of a new day in your development as a coach. You have been given this day as a gift that you can open with joy or you can waste it. You are exchanging a day of your life for it. When tomorrow's sun comes up today's practice will be gone forever. Make this day valuable, so you can grow, so you can gain and not lose. You must pay a price in effort and attitude and focus if you want today to be a success and not a failure. Do your best today and you will not fail. You cannot fail when you give your best effort. Today is the very first day of the rest of your coaching life.

Make this a goal: Not to be better than anyone else, but to be better tomorrow than you are today.

I will do it.
I will do it right.
I will do it right now.

Concerns and doubts may have held you back because of lack of focus. Those doubts can be erased if you focus on what you need to do today. In this way the excessive beating of your heart and your pre-game jitters in life will lessen and help you become a great coach.

Polishing the Nugget

Pre-game jitters used to get to me as I handled all the details of away games. I was also the athletic director, so getting the bus, pre-game meal arrangements, tickets, game plans, after-game eating, making sure all the players got on the bus on time, ran through my head.

The 'old coach' in me had a rule that if you were late, the bus would leave without you. I knew another coach who told me he would wait in a bar across the street until all the players had arrived, then someone would come and get him. Not me! I was there early and ready to leave.

I'd just told the driver to head out when we all heard a voice yell, "Wait! Wait!" A player was running for the bus. I told the bus driver to shut the door, "Let's go." He must have had a son who played because he hesitated just long enough to let Roger jump on. Of course I was angry.

The entire team sat in silence, wondering how I would react, when the player, totally out of breath, managed to say, "I'm sorry. I was here earlier, but realized I'd forgotten my prosthetic toe."

I looked at him in wonder as I remembered him telling me about a lawn mower accident that summer. I needed to make a decision: Do it. Do it right. Do it right now.

I said, "OK, get on the bus." I turned and looked at the rest of the players and said, "If any of you are late for the bus because of your prosthetic toe, you will get a waiver. Roger just used his! OK, let's get this bus rolling."

I heard snickers, saw lots of smiles and some high fives for Roger as he sat down.

Do it. Do it right. Do it right now.

From the Office—Coach Faylor

"With each responsibility, do it right."

—Everett Dean, Indiana University coach

From the Locker Room—Little K

"Right's right even if nobody's doing it.

Wrong's wrong even if everybody's doing it.
I will take action to do right today."

—Donald L. McKendry, John Glenn
High School principal (Ohio)

Start today. Help your players learn how to dribble a ball with either hand while being able to see the entire floor at the same time. Accept all coaching duties. See your players for who they are and the potential they possess. Help them focus on what they need to do to become better, not just in basketball but in life.

I will do it.
I will do it right.
I will do it right now.

Action speaks louder than words, even though you must also believe in the power of words. When you enter the gymnasium each day, say the following words and immediately encourage and lift the players.

I will do it.
I will do it right.
I will do it right now.

Sometimes you'll want to stop practice and toss the players out of the gym for the day because of poor performance, lack of patience or anger. When you feel this way, remind yourself that you have lost focus. You must take a deep breath and say, "Do it. Do it right. Do it right now." Then find ways to make practice better and end the day on a positive note.

I will do it.
I will do it right.
I will do it right now.

Prepare when other coaches seek rest. Talk when other coaches remain silent. Your actions will be evident even when you choose to remain quiet, for it will be a choice to act wisely, showing your strength of mind and character. Select your words wisely so they augment your actions.

Work with players after practice; most other coaches can't find the time. Stay each day until all the needs of your players are fulfilled. It will never be too late to act, to help, to finish with the players when other coaches would say that it's time to leave.

I will do it.
I will do it right.
I will do it right now.

I am not a dreamer. I am a dream doer. I will do it right now.

Polishing the Nugget

A player stops in to talk about an academic problem. I'm busy and say, "Come back tomorrow." He leaves school that night.

My daughter calls and wants to know if I'm coming home for her birthday party. I say, "I'm busy, but I will try my best." I don't make it. When I said "yes" to something else, I said "no" to my daughter!

Time rules all of us. And we all have the same number of hours each day. You must focus and constantly re-focus on what you know is truly most important in life. Being blinded by the never-ending duties of coaching will cause you to lose focus with your players and your family.

Do it. Do it right. Do it right now.

You need to have a tremendous desire to become a great coach. You must want to achieve and want to help your players achieve. You want to be a good parent and husband also.

You want to be the best you can become. These are all just words unless you act. Unless you act, you will not succeed.

Your actions will be seen by your players and family and they will be lifted into action.

Victory can come on the floor, but get lost in the office with a player or at home with a child. **This** is the moment to do it. **This** is the place to do it right. You can become the greatest coach today by doing it right now.

From the Office—Coach Faylor

"One must count each day a separate life."

—Seneca

What will you focus on today?

I will do it.
I will do it right.
I will do it right now.
I will blow my golden whistle today.

To the Reader

Congratulations on finishing the eighth nugget. Your ideas, your knowledge and your thoughts are great only if you can turn them into action.

1. What is the theme of nugget 8?

2. What is the mantra?

3. What's the Big Word?

4. Is it ok to react negatively?

5. What is a takeaway from this nugget that will help you be a better coach?

6. Snap your fingers and it's gone, but it will determine your fate. If you want the Golden Whistle, don't wait. It may already be too late. What am I?

GOLDEN NUGGET NO. 9

My Way or the Highway

Relationships

I believe that your ability to make an emotional connection with
people so that you both lift each other is paramount. It must
become a partnership where there is synergism on both sides. In
today's changing world a coach at any level will need to develop
great relationships with all the people involved in his program.

Learn to relate.

Believe it or not basketball coaching, like most things in
life, requires you to develop relationship skills. Some
coaches just don't seem to get this. They think they can do it
all and not need to rely on other people. A lot of them don't
even think they need a good relationship with their players.
This attitude is a killer if you are in coaching for the long haul.
One of the differences between where you are now and where
you want to be will be the people you meet and the relationships you develop and maintain. I realized early in my career
that relationship development must be a priority to work on
every day.

As coaching has evolved from its very infant stage, there
are more and more coaches with egos that are bigger even
than the schools they represent. They think the game revolves
around them. Their egos make having solid relationships very
difficult. I realize that you need a pretty big ego to coach, but
you must be able to get along with the people involved and
develop positive, enduring relationships.

The first priority is to develop a good relationship with your players. The old coaching idea, 'It's my way or the highway,' is slowly becoming a thing of the past. The ability to understand the 'whole' player as a student and as a player and as a person is paramount. I will be the first to tell you that today's players need discipline and they need to be tougher, but they also need to know that you trust and care about them. They will drive you crazy, disappoint you at times and leave you speechless with their immaturity. You must still be able to relate to the players and understand the changes they are going through.

Are you truly interested in the players or are you interested more in how you can use them to win and get a better job? It's important to first know who you are before finding out who they are; then you have a chance to relate.

DO YOU REALLY KNOW YOUR PLAYERS?

1. Do you ask about their family?

2. Do they have a boyfriend or girlfriend?

3. How are they doing academically?

4. What do they like to do in their spare time?

5. What problems or concerns do they have?

6. Do you know their life and career aspirations?

7. Can they talk to you? More importantly, can you talk to them?

A great question to ask is, "How's Mom and Dad?" I've known coaches from all levels who don't like to even **talk** with parents. Some coaches view parents as the enemy and the less contact the better. I was blessed to have great parents and became friends for life with many of them. Of course you must be careful and not base playing time on these friendships.

Relationships with parents are based on a simple premise: they love their child more than they love you.

Moms love their children more than they love you. She is sending you her most important possession. She is saying to you, "I'm giving you my child. Help me make him better not only as a player, but as a person. I'm giving you my child to develop. Please send him back a man."

Polishing the Nugget

Relationship-building is paramount in a large family. I had six brothers and sisters. We were very poor but very loving and very proud. We lived in a very small house with a pot-bellied coal stove and an outhouse. There was one bedroom downstairs (for mom and dad) and one and a half bedrooms upstairs (for the rest of us.) The seven of us, four girls and three boys, slept in one large bedroom.

I was the oldest boy and had three older sisters who gave me a lot of love and a lot of grief. Hand-me-downs were common and that's how I became so tough. I had to wear my sisters' saddle shoes and training bras. I got into a lot of fights. Oh, yes. I was just kidding about the training bra.

The evening at bedtime reminded me of the Waltons. We would hear "Good night, Sue," "Good night, Joyce," Good night, Barb," "Good night, Jim" then someone would giggle, we would start over and Dad would yell, "Settle down! You don't want me coming up there."

We were a great band of wild youngsters and my mom loved all of us the best. Mom was the armed guard on the wild wagon full of kids she loved and related to. In our house we could pick on each other, but you had to fight us all if you picked on one of us at school.

> With both Mom and Dad it wasn't ever "My way or the highway." It was, "Our way down the highway." The best relationships are built on love.

I have received some letters, notes, phone calls and even visits from parents (and others) with messages that are demeaning to my coaching and character. I read them, address them, then throw them away and try to develop a better relationship with the person. What a great challenge: to relate to people who think you can't coach a lick! You can do this by believing in yourself, not taking assaults too personally and having great patience.

I have also had a lot of encouraging messages. I keep these and embellish the people who send them. They are easy to relate to, easy to like, easy to develop lifetime relations with.

I like the notes that say positive, inspiring things, like the note I received from a dad about his son returning for his senior year. The son told his father, "Dad, I'm going back to school to build mountains." (He was referring to helping his team win a championship.) The dad wrote that to me and went on to tell me, "I knew I had sent a boy to play for you and I have a man there now. Thanks for helping him from boyhood to manhood, God's greatest gift."

I have a relationship with that family to this day, but it is easy because we share positive relationships. Our way is the best way.

Polishing the Nugget

I developed a lifelong relationship with a fan from just a casual meeting at a basketball game.

A woman and her husband, Frank, approached me at the game. She said that her father loved our team and that he was dying of cancer and she just wanted to tell me that he never missed a game. I took off my hat and signed it and said, "Please tell him I said thanks for being such a great fan."

Two weeks later I received this letter: "I'm extremely sorry this letter is so late, but things have been hectic in the past two weeks. My wife and I would like to thank you for the ball cap you autographed for my father-in-law. When my wife gave it to him, he could not fight the tears that overcame him. Of course he wore it to bed. My wife had never before initiated a conversation with a stranger as she did with you, but she wasn't exaggerating when she said how much he loved watching your team. In fact, it was one of the few things he really looked forward to watching on television. This morning, my father-in-law passed away. He was a spunky guy with great courage and a lot of heart. I'm sure this is why he enjoyed your play so much. Thanks for your kindness. It helped my father-in-law with those last few days and will help my wife and me forever."

Frank and I have remained friends for the past thirty years and just recently have begun following each other's blogs (http://coachjess.hoopsource.com.) Your kindness can make a difference in others' lives.

How do you travel down the highway? I can tell you from experience that you never know where your influence ends. You never know where great relationships can begin. Be ready!

There are four levels of relationships that, in coaching, we all need to be aware of.

1. Warm-up Relationships (Short-Term)

These are acquaintances, people you meet and move past, players who come and go, parents of players you recruited but didn't get; yes, those types of relationships. There is not a lot of interaction or frequency of meeting, but your ability to develop relations even with these people during the brief time you know them is paramount to your success. You are planting seeds for life.

2. Turnover Relationships (Short-Term)

Lose-Win. The people you are playing against in the game and in life seem to keep taking advantage of you and denying you the things you love most. You usually get short-changed in this relationship and it is defined as lose-win. The coaches on the other team that beat you and 'take' your championship away. Can you have a relationship with them? Can you find a way to love them anyway?

3. Steals Relationships (Short-Term)

Win-Lose. This is just the opposite of number two. In these relationships, you always seem to be asking for more, wanting more and getting more. Win-lose situation. If you win, you steal others' contributions by making people think it was all you. You are not helping players develop, parents to get involved, assistants to become better. Can they love you anyway?

4. Assist Relationships (Long-Term)

Win-Win. You provide something for the players and they give it back. You love the parents, they love you. You make a great pass as a player, your teammate scores, winks at you and gives you a high five. This is based on mutual love, respect and loyalty. Everyone involved gives and gets. Remember, "Giving Gets." Can we love each other? Ralph Waldo Emerson once wrote, "A great gift has to be a portion of yourself—give freely, receive freely."

My way or the highway
or
Our way is the best way.
Which will it be for you?

Relationships can be built on the Big Word Offense:

TRUST
LOYALTY
TRUSTWORTHINESS   **RELATIONSHIPS**
APPRECIATION
COMMITMENT
SINCERITY
OPENNESS
COMPASSION
RESPONSIBILITY
GENEROSITY
FLEXIBILITY   What is your relationship goal?
DEPENDABILITY
RESPECTFULNESS

Relationships are built on trust and loyalty. Remember, it's not just what you know but who you **really** know and who **really** knows you. Make friends on the way up so you have someone to soften the fall on the way down.

'My way or the highway' just doesn't develop great relationships. Believe me, I know. I coached like that for years. I understand that it takes a lot to develop and maintain your relationships with players and parents in the competitive environment of coaching, but it doesn't stop there. You must also relate to the media, to the administration, to the fans and boosters and alumni, to the officials and to your opponents. What a great challenge, one that I accepted and embraced over the years, and I challenge you to do the same. You can't say, "That's just the way I am."

Try to create an image of yourself and your program that you can be proud of and that the school can also look up to. Fill your Relationship Travel Bag with:

1. **A Smile**—This is a great gift to have and to give. Ask, "How can I help you?" when you first meet someone.

2. **A Listening Badge**. (Not 'my way or the highway') "How can I help you?"

3. **Ability and Desire to meet people.**

4. **Respect** all opponents, all people.

5. **A Note Pad.** Take notes. A pen and a business card. Write a note on each business card you receive, something that helps you really remember the person and situation.

6. **The Big Word Offense**—Grow your vocabulary so you can relate to a diverse group. It's great against any full court press.

7. It's a **Back Court Violation Rule** if you don't introduce yourself and ask, "How can I help you" within ten seconds of meeting someone.

8. **Relationship Currency**. The cost of building relationships. You need to wisely spend some of the following:

   ✓ Time

   ✓ Energy

✓ Ideas

✓ Loyalty

9. Get a **T-Shirt** that says, "Make me feel important" or a sign that says, "Relate." My Big Offense Word for next year is relate.

The challenge for developing relationships with your players will be realized if later they recognize you as one of the most influential people in their lives. What a great challenge and a great way to coach.

My way or the highway
or
Our way down the highway.

You get to decide.

Relationships are hard to teach, but they must be encouraged by every coach who wants the team to become all they can become. Coaching is about taking care of the people you call players. It's a people business, not just a basketball game business.

'Put the ball in the basket' and 'Stop the other team' are great goals. Put your energy and passion into the game. But put your heart and soul into your relationships with your players. That is where you will find the formula to success.

When you can get twelve players to come together, to put away selfish attitudes and problems and play for each other, you have the right to call yourself a coach and ask, "Where's that Golden Whistle?"

The secret: there is no secret, other than getting better every year that you teach and coach and challenging your players to do the same. Relate—Relate—Relate!

Find a way to keep your best players, even if they are challenging, and surround them with great role players and an understanding bench.

Learn to relate.
　　The bench, the bench, my court for a bench!*

To the Reader

Congratulations on finishing the ninth nugget.

1.　What is the theme of nugget 9?

2.　What is the mantra?

3.　What's the Big Word?

4.　Why is developing relationships important in coaching?

---

*　　This is a paraphrase of "A horse, a horse, my kingdom for a horse!" from *Richard III* by William Shakespeare.

GOLDEN NUGGET NO. 10

Lord, I Ask That You Bless Me Indeed

Gratitude

Gratitude is the ability to feel thankfulness no matter what circumstances you find yourself in. When you have and when you don't have; when you get what you expected and when you get nothing that you expected. True gratitude arrives equally in all circumstances. This is a great time to coach. Thank you.

Coaching can change a coach's mood and demeanor about as quickly as any profession in the world. I realized early that I needed a higher purpose so I could stay on the positive trail toward constant improvement in my coaching career. I needed to be more appreciative, more thankful. I needed to adjust and, yes, even change the way I responded to all the situations and circumstances that come with coaching. Very slowly I developed gratitude moments where, in the midst of chaos I learned to say, "Thank you." I found, quite simply, the best way to stay focused and move ahead was to express gratitude with a very sincere "Thank you."

THE LANGUAGE OF GRATITUDE

The grammar of gratitude is quite easy. A simple "thank you" will do. Even a warmly-expressed "I appreciate you" will bring a smile to the face of most people. "May you have many blessings" encourages relationships to be formed. By blessing others, we are blessed ourselves.

Coaching is a tough, competitive environment. Work hard, be tough, discipline the players because in your heart you know they need it and want it. But constantly remind yourself, "We are teaching and coaching for and with the players." The language is simple: "Thank you."

From the Classroom—Coach Aupp

"What you are to be
you are now becoming."

—Robert Montgomery,
Muskingum University president

THE SPECTRUM OF GRATITUDE

Do I hear a roller coaster? The ups and downs of coaching can go from greed and need and jealousy—"I want more," "I need more," "You are killing our team"—to acceptance and appreciation—"What a great effort in practice today. Thank you."

The ego is often ungrateful. It always seems to demand more if you let it have its way:

When we win, it says, "You're great. We need more wins."

When we play well, it says, "Not good enough."

When we lose, of course Mr. Ego says, "Not my fault."

In coaching, these emotions will come into play every day. It is only natural to react, but you must prepare yourself, because in basketball emotions change on each possession. Practice hard, lead the team, care about the players and be grateful for being allowed to coach.

"Bull crap!" you say. That's the response of ego's ingratitude, and it is natural to feel these things. As a coach you must discipline yourself to react with class and with a simple "Thank you."

Lord, bless me indeed.

GRATITUDE CHECK

Give yourself a quick check of your gratitude level. When you lose, can you be appreciative and thankful toward the other coach and his players? Can you stand by with class and let the winners pass? You lead your players not by what you say but by what you do when it counts.

Pass the class!

INGRATITUDE

The intention of true gratitude is to be thankful every day, even and especially when you lose at the buzzer. The whining, "We got cheated!" and "Why does this always happen to me?" and "Our players suck!" seem to surface more quickly than gratitude. It is often easier to have a sense of "Why me?" ingratitude and blame everyone else.

Ingratitude is really a sense of feeling sorry for ourselves and it makes us feel better by finding excuses why we lost. A good coach prepares himself for these moments by how he responds every day in practice.

Experience is a tough teacher. She gives you the test first and the lessons later. Start preparing for the tests today. A simple "Thank you" is always a great place to start.

I know, I know. This is all easy to say but tough to do. As a coach you must set the example anyway. Be tough, be hard, work their butts off, but be thankful they are your players.

Give thanks for a little and you just may get a lot!

THREE LANGUAGES

I am fluent in three languages: basketball, English and body language and I have a minor in the Big Word Offense.

A simple nod or wink or smile to a player after he made a great pass for a layup or took a charge can lift the spirits of all the players during a game. As a coach, you expect that kind of camaraderie* from your players. But you need to read your own body language too. A positive reaction when one of your players makes a big turnover for a tense situation expresses gratitude and confidence in the player. Conversely, a pouty reaction, shoulder-slumping, glaring at a player or jerking him out of the game can be devastating to the team's morale.

A frown or glare or negative reaction can restrict and fan fear into players who make mistakes. A smile or pat on the back can lift all the players to continue to give their best.

Body language speaks loud and clear. Pass the class.

It is a soft shot indeed that bounces on the rim two, three, four times before it tumbles in or out. It is a good coach indeed who can give an expression of gratitude with just how he looks when it bounces in or out. Are you fluent in body language?

THE GRATITUDE CHALLENGE

I too used to say, "That's just the way I am" and "That's just the way I react" and even "I'm too old to change." Well, I challenge you as a coach to always teach and coach your players better and always believe they can get better. Never accept in yourself or with your team that this is 'just' the way it is. We **can and must** as coaches continue to be grateful for what we have and hopeful that we can become more.

"Thank you" brings out the best.

> ### Polishing the Nugget
>
> The death of my parents changed my attitude and gratitude. Prior to that, I'd be concerned when friends' parents passed away; I'd send a card or call or even go to calling hours.
>
> But when my parents passed away within six months of each other, I felt the pain and hurt and watched people

* If you can't give a clear definition of this word to another person, look it up. Then use it in tomorrow's practice with your players.

travel from all over to come to the funeral. It was then that I made up my mind and changed my attitude to one of really caring.

I would miss practice, I would take extra time, I would stay afterward to console and help in any way I could. This is particularly important with your players, who often will lose grandparents during their time on your team. Showing that you care, showing your support is a way of saying, "Thank you for all you have done for me. I deeply appreciate it."

Change your attitude with genuine gratitude.

From the Office—Coach Faylor

"Therefore, be at peace with God, whatever you conceive Him to be, and whatever your labors and aspirations, in the noisy confusion of life keep peace with your soul. With all its sham, drudgery and broken dreams, it is still a beautiful world. Be careful. Strive to be happy."

—Max Ehrmann, *Desiderata*

Engage these words as a coach. Put these beautiful words from *Desiderata* to memory. (Yes you **can** memorize it.) It will help shape your career.

Follow your coaching dreams. It's a great time to coach. Strive to be happy. Pursue the Golden Whistle.

THE PRAYER OF JABEZ

No matter how many years I coached, there were always those moments late in the game when the score was tied, the ball was in the air, we were playing against a great opponent; in those moments I would say, "Lord, please let this go in." Who has not shed tears of joy after a big win and pointed toward the heavens and said, "Thank you." We have all sought help from a power beyond us.

During my moments of joy and despair in coaching, I found comfort in the words of Jabez' prayer from *I Chronicles 4:9-10* in the Bible*. The passage from my King James version reads, "Lord, I ask that you bless me indeed, that you extend my territory that you will put your hand in mine and that you will keep me from evil."

Be grateful. Be grateful. Be grateful.

It's a simple sentence but contains four profound concepts that have helped me immensely. I'd like to share them with you.

1. Lord, I would ask that you bless me indeed.

It might be easier for an old coach to ask, "Lord, I hope you let me win." But just as winning takes a lot of preparation and hard work, asking for blessings comes with a responsibility that you deserve to be blessed in the way that you've requested.

It certainly doesn't hurt late in the game, with the score tied and the ball in the air to yell out, "Lord, bless me indeed!" But we both know it won't make much difference. God doesn't care who wins, only how blessed you feel just to be a part of the game. Oh, he will bless you indeed; go ahead and ask often, but he will bless you if you have earned it.

2. That you would extend my territory.

You will always need to grow as a coach and as a person. The more you extend your knowledge of the game and yourself, the more you can impart to the players. You may thank God for extending your winning streak and thank Him for your Coach of the Year honors, but what comes with that is the responsibility to give Him the credit and realize that expectations soar and the ante goes up as you increase your territory.

---

*   Note from Coach Faylor: This was explored deeply in the best-selling book, *The Prayer of Jabez*, by Bruce Wilkinson (2000).

3. That you put your hand in my hand.

After a tough loss, an argument with an official or confrontation with parents, I often held out my hand and asked Him to put His hand in mine. He never failed to respond. Of course you must believe in your team. You must believe in your players. You must believe in yourself and believe in a power higher than yourself. Reach out and feel your hand in His.

Pass the class

4. And that you would keep me from evil.

If you don't want to eat sweets, then you should not keep them around. If you feel the temptation to do something that is not right, challenge yourself, but the best way is to stay away from the temptation.

In coaching, it is sometimes easy to blame others, to swear, to rant and rave at injustices, but it might be as easy as not putting yourself into damaging situations and learning not to react negatively. Then you have a chance to be kept from evil.

Whatever you conceive God to be, whatever you believe, Jabez' prayer can bring you peace; and in coaching, there will be moments we all seek peace!

It is a great time to [coach basketball].
Insert your own area of focus within the brackets.

A good coach who seeks the Golden Whistle must work hard and believe in his system and pass that to all those around him. I call this:

PASS AROUND THE GRATEFUL

When a new person approaches, **smile** a lot.

When times get tough, learn to be **hopeful.**

When you feel cheated by bad calls, **embrace** the officials.

When you are too tired to go on, **be thankful** that you have come this far.

When someone pushes your helping hand away, **extend** your other hand.

When your team loses, **be glad** for the **joy** of the other team.

When a loss hurts so deeply you feel like dying, let the **smile** you receive from friends and family bring you back.

When you are down and your team is reeling, being **thankful** you have each other may be enough.

When you go into the locker room after a game, win or lose, look your players in the eye and say, **"Thank you** for letting me coach you tonight."

What you have today are the things you used to hope for. **Be grateful** for what you have.

When you lose, the sun will still come up the next day. Go back to practice; you will find **joy** based on how you cope with your loss.

You may not have the season you want, but if you handled it with **class** you can **be proud and grateful.**

Be grateful for being a coach, for all the great people in your life.

Pass the class.

Be grateful and pass the class. I hope that you will still get after your players push them, work them, challenge them and also lift them to places they dream to be. Oh, they will disappoint you once in awhile, but you must believe in them, help them, correct them, stand by them and lift them. Show them with your actions how much you care, then say, "Thank you. I appreciate you. Let's do this together."

Get a gratitude attitude.
Lord, you have blessed me indeed.

Pursue your Golden Whistle, but remember, it's a whistle. It will not turn to gold on its own. It's not a magic whistle.

Your desire, your dreams, your pursuit of the Golden Whistle and becoming a great coach is admirable indeed, but you must blow the whistle yourself.

It's a great time to coach.
Blow your whistle!

To the Reader

Congratulations on finishing the tenth and final nugget.

1. What is the theme of nugget 10?

2. What is the mantra?

3. What's the Big Word?

4. Do you have a gratitude attitude?

5. Why did I mention a roller coaster?

EPILOGUE

The Banquet

Faylor Returns—Three Years Later

Coach Faylor walked toward the arena, reflecting on how it had been over the past three years since his retirement from coaching. Most of his thoughts were good, but he had to admit that he missed the practices and the close relationship with the players. However, when he thought of the long, arduous seasons, the tough practices, scouting, long recruiting trips, media presentations and public relations demands he knew that he did not have the energy to coach anymore.

He had walked this quadrangle so many times before and he was particularly excited about this basketball banquet. It would be a very special event. Little K had just won his first national championship in his third year as head coach; Jay, his high school freshman star, was helping him as a student assistant while working on his master's degree.

Faylor opened the door to the arena and walked into the cavernous gymnasium. He was early as usual—they were just finishing the set-up. The floor was covered with tarp; a hundred or more tables and chairs were all set up for the banquet. The coach could feel it full of 21,000 screaming fans. He looked up and saw his picture hanging from the rafters along with those great players whose numbers had been retired. As he reflected on those times, he noticed another banner that was covered up; he smiled and thought, *Little K certainly deserves this honor.* Last year Big K's picture had been added alongside his, which filled him with pride as well as bringing a tear of happiness for his old friend. This was the first time that an assistant coach had been honored with a place in the university's hall of fame.

But the ache in his heart was deeper than that. Faylor stood in silence and shuddered at the thought of losing his dear wife of fifty years just a month earlier. She had battled cancer for the past three years and she continued to lift and support the people around her right up until the end. He reflected that we often don't realize what we have until we lose it. But he knew and had always known that he had the best wife and the best coach's wife who had ever lived. Period.

The white-haired coach was startled from his reverie by a bump in the back. He turned and saw the smiling face of Little K, who said, "You looked lost in deep thought. Hey, you look in great shape. I can tell you're not sitting around eating cookies and watching TV. Thanks for coming tonight. It makes me feel really special to have you attend. You taught me Faylor time. I guess that's why I'm here so early. You never know when they might need some help setting up."

The younger coach then took the hand of his mentor and friend and said, "I know we saw each other at the funeral, but I want you to know how sad I still am about your wife's death. Sonie was such an amazing woman and was the best role model for any coach's wife. At the funeral I remembered things about her that I'd forgotten: that she was a piano major in college with aspirations of becoming a professional, but she gave that up to marry you and have a family.

"She was always a giver to the players, to her church and her friends. Her volunteering was legendary, and her class, patience and caring endeared her to all the people she ever met. My heart goes out to you in your loss. It must have been difficult for you to come tonight without her. You know you're among family here, though, and we all understand."

Faylor squeezed Little K's hand tightly and turned his head away to hide his tears and said softly, "Thanks, Little K. You always know what to say. I really appreciate that. Sonie was a remarkable lady and she taught me a lot about how to relate to people. She never met anyone she didn't like. I will always miss her, but she was adamant near the end that I continue to live my life, so I will honor her request. It feels good to be here."

Little K squeezed back, then changed to a lighter note as the two left the arena and returned to the entry hall. "By the way, Big K has been in Florida playing golf and flew back to be here tonight. I must say that he really knows how to enjoy retirement. Did you know he has a girlfriend? Well, you probably do. Can you imagine?" Both men smiled, then laughed, hugged each other and cried.

"On another note," continued Little K after blowing his nose, "Do you remember Myron, my player who went to Harvard? His dad just retired last week but said he'll still sing in the Christmas pageant. His mom has a couple of years left, but she's working on a book about Myron's experience at Harvard and being selected as a Rhodes scholar. You were right. It's not about winning, but about helping young people become more than they even thought they could be."

Little K looked at his mentor and snapped his fingers. "I know I've told you this before, but thank you. I can't tell you how much those two years in high school helped mold and develop me into a coach. I had no idea what it took. I really learned how to be humble, and yet despite the difficulties it somehow strengthened my resolve that I could become a coach after all. It was your faith in me, your support and encouragement that kept me in the game. And your Golden Nuggets have sustained me every day I live. I can never thank you enough."

Faylor stopped him, saying, "You did it on your own. I just opened the door a little. My challenge for you hasn't changed. I want you to continue to grow as a coach, to continue to help and mentor young coaches and to share the nuggets with anyone who wants to become better. I don't know if it's easier or harder today, but I know you must continue to be passionate about coaching and work hard.

"Congratulations on the new ebook you just published. It gives great new insights to coaching. Everybody can strive to become great, but few will achieve that status. Keep doing what you've been doing; change, adjust, but keep your basic values. You've earned your Golden Whistle, but remember; you have to earn it again next year."

Little K's response, "Don't I know it!" was interrupted by a familiar voice calling, "Do you think we are a little early?" Big K, wearing a huge grin, was striding quickly toward them across the lobby floor, holding the hand of a statuesque grey-haired woman. The two coaches walked toward the pair and met them in the middle. Big K, attempting to sound casual, said, "I'd like to introduce you to my friend Joanna."

Faylor and Little K both ignored Joanna's outstretched hand, preferring to skip the formalities and greet her with bear hugs, followed by hugs and back slaps with Big K. The foursome began to chat and both Faylor and Little K quickly realized that Big K had found a gem in Joanna.

After a few minutes Little K said, "I hate to interrupt this when we're just getting acquainted but Jackie, my assistant, just beeped me. And I see that they're beginning to let the guests in. I guess it's about time for the banquet."

He snapped his fingers and said, "Let's go do this." They all smiled as Little K held the big door and the four friends stepped into the gym and walked toward the podium.

Little K was quickly surrounded by staff members who had last-minute instructions and questions. His assistant led the other three to their seats at the VIP table near the front. A steady stream of friends and former colleagues made their way to their table to say hello to the well-liked retired coaches. Over the next forty-five minutes guests continued to arrive until every seat was full. Then the lights flashed to signal the beginning of the ceremony and the audience became quiet.

The athletic director introduced the dignitaries and then introduced Little K. The response was thunderous. Everybody loves a winner. Little K spoke, "Thank you, ladies and gentlemen. What a great night for our basketball program and our university. Winning a national championship is beyond my wildest dreams and we are here tonight to celebrate! I would call this a golden moment."

"Before we get into the awards, I would like Coach Faylor to come up to the podium." This took the senior coach by surprise, but he walked to the front. Little K continued, "We have a special award, a real golden moment, that I want to share. Coach Faylor, I think you noticed the new banner hanging from the rafters. I am certain that you thought it was for the national championship team or even thought it might be for me. However, the university board of trustees and the administration have all agreed that tonight we unveil another member of our hall of fame. Someone who earned the Golden Whistle many times over. I am proud beyond words to unveil this tonight. Next year, at the start of the season, we will do it formally."

"Coach, on behalf of all of us, please take this rope and pull the canvas down. I think this is a first, but we wanted your wife, Sonie, to hang beside you, along with Big K. She earned her Golden Whistle. God bless you, Coach."

There was a long, almost deafening silence as Coach Faylor drew down the rope. As the picture was unveiled, the audience erupted into loud, enthusiastic cheering, whistles, and a standing ovation. At a gesture from Little K, Big K walked up onto the stage and the three men embraced.

What a great moment. What a great time to be a coach's wife. What a great time to be an assistant coach.

The wins and losses are important, but the Big Word Offense never grows old and still trumps them all. Love and caring, giving and sharing, the words that turn your life to gold.

How will you earn your Golden Whistle? How will you live your life? Remember, only you can blow your whistle.

What a great time to coach. Go for the Gold!

ACKNOWLEDGMENTS

Coaches—Don McKillip, Marysville Junior High School; Bob Tucker, Marysville High School; Ed Sherman (football) and Bob Burkholder (basketball) Muskingum University.

Coaching friends—John McClendon, mentor; Page Moir, friend and colleague (Roanoke College men's head coach); George Klein (Muskingum University assistant coach); George Raveling, life teacher, friend and mentor (Nike Director of International Basketball); Andy Clark, always willing to help with his great mind (Muskingum University assistant coach).

Teacher—Delbert Oberteuffer (Ohio State University professor), the best teacher I ever had; the reason I taught my classes the way I did was because of this man.

Nike—Elite Youth Basketball League (EYBL) and Coaches Learning Academy—who hired me when I retired from Muskingum and who continues to believe in me.

Mike Crowley, founder and CEO of 94Fifty, who hired me and my son Jay as consultants and has enriched my life in both business and technology.

Friends—Pat Campbell, 'Super Scout', who has lifted my heart for the past fifty years; Jim Arganbright and Les Baum, for their dedication and desire to always help–they were the true basketball camp directors for thirty-plus unforgettable years; Joe Arganbright, a guide, a friend and co-conspirator for a long time.

All my players and their parents who supported our program at Muskingum. You made it a great run. From All-Americans to the bench players, thank you all for being great role models.

All my assistant coaches, who carried me at all times, I can't thank you enough.

Book helpers—Judy Haselhoef, who shared many insights while writing her own book, *Give and Take: Doing Our Damnedest to NOT Create a Charity in Haiti;* Rebecca Mullen, the gifted author coach, who lifted my heart and spirit when they faltered and helped shape the book; Jane Varley, Professor of English at Muskingum University, friend and neighbor, who edited and improved the book; Mike Bruny, for giving us the "hungry coach" concept.

Dan Weeks and Betsy Rapoport—Although neither one edited this book, they each gave me critical early input that defined and shaped the final product more than they could ever have imagined. (Pamela Slim, thank you so much for the introduction to Betsy.)

JetLaunch for the book production and helping us navigate the wild new world of self-publishing digital books.

My real head coaches—Sondra Kaye Saam Burson for 40 wonderful years of support and love until 1999; Jennifer Sue Lyle (Burson), who has shaped my life and is my main inspiration for completing this book. They both have loved, shared and given much. They both have blessed me indeed and earned their Golden Whistles.

My children and grandchildren, Jamie (Madison and Margo) and Jay (Lee, Ty and Jess), who continue to amaze me.

My mom and dad, who loved me for who I was and challenged me to become more.

My brothers and sisters Joyce, Sue, Barbara, Judy, Steve and John, who allowed me to grow up feeling love and joy.

My New Concord crew—Gary and Pegge Bradley, Bill and Emilie Geyer, Larry and Betty Miller, Don and Jean McKendry, Tim and Karen Messerschmidt, Doc and Marcia Chess, George and Martha Graham; you are all life-enhancers. A special thanks to Geoff and Jim Vejsicky—I've been blessed to know the father and the son.

The National Association of Basketball Coaches (NABC), Guardians of the Game—thank you for my life membership and permitting me the honor of serving on the board and as president.

The NCAA, who allowed me to serve as national chair of Division III basketball.

All the Division III coaches who are earning their Golden Whistles the hard way—they have worked their butts off for them!

The Ohio Basketball Hall of Fame—Doc Daugherty and Don Henderson, both master coaches and gentlemen.

Grant Wahl, for including me in his great *Sports Illustrated* article on Pete Carill and the Princeton Offense.

Bobby Knight, who allowed me to help with the 1984 Olympic trials.

Muskingum University for my B. A. and The Ohio State University for my M.A. and PhD. They molded a young student into a life-long learner.

And to anyone I've left out, I am sorry. It's like sitting on the bench and not getting in the game, but be assured that I love you anyway.

THANK YOU FOR READING!

Dear Reader,

Thanks for reading *The Golden Whistle*.

I've read a lot of basketball books—all of them were valuable, but the ones that truly helped develop me as a coach were the ones I engaged with.

What do I mean by 'engage'? This is my ten-step engagement process for learning by reading:

1. Read the book all the way through.

2. Mark areas and phrases that really catch my attention.

3. Write questions in the margins.

4. Use a dictionary to look up and define any terms I'm not clear about.

5. Outline the book on paper, using a pen or pencil, not computer. This doesn't necessarily follow a formal academic outlining structure, but I do include all sections of the book in my notes.

6. Study other writings by the author.

7. Contact the author by phone or with a note to ask for any clarification I need.

8. Write down my answers to any questions that the author has posed at the end of chapters or sections.

9. Have friends or assistant coaches read the same book and discuss what might be helpful for us. **This may be the most important step in the process—connect with other coaches.**

10. At the end of this process, I may have added only one or two things, but they have always made a difference because I believed in them.

Coaches always love after-the-game evaluations. If there is something you really liked or were not clear on, please let me know. I'd welcome the opportunity for further engagement with you. You can email me at **jim@jimburson.com** and visit my website, Solution-Based Basketball® **www.jimburson.com**. I'll be adding free *Golden Whistle* resources and materials there over time.

Want to go a step further? Please review the book on Amazon. I'd sincerely appreciate it and a couple of sentences from you would go a long way in helping other potential readers. **http://amazon.com/author/jimburson**

Are you engaging the game and actively pursuing your own Golden Whistle every day? Good luck!

Yours in great basketball,

Dr. Jim Burson

Free newsletter and blog at Jim Burson's Solution-Based Basketball®: **http://jimburson.com/free-updates**

Bulk sales of *The Golden Whistle* for your team or organization: **info@jimburson.com**

Made in the USA
Charleston, SC
18 September 2014